Montana Writers' Cookbook

EAT OUR WORDS

Sharon,
Merry Christmas 2009!
Grant picked this
especially for you.
Enjoy,
Grant, Ron & Pam

compiled by Montana Center for the Book • Montana Committee for the Humanities

FARCOUNTRY
PRESS

ISBN-13: 978-1-56037-341-4
ISBN-10: 1-56037-341-5

© 2005 Farcountry Press
Text © 2005 Montana Committee for the Humanities

For more information on our books, write Farcountry Press, P.O. Box 5630, Helena, MT 59604; call (800) 821-3874; or visit www.farcountrypress.com.

Created, produced, and designed in the United States.
Printed in Canada.

10 09 08 07 06 05   1 2 3 4 5 6

Library of Congress Cataloging-in-Publication Data

Eat our words : the Montana writers cookbook / compiled by Montana Center for the Book,
Montana Committee for the Humanities.
p. cm.
Includes index.
ISBN-13: 978-1-56037-341-4
ISBN-10: 1-56037-341-5
1. Cookery, American. 2. Cookery--Montana. I. Montana Center for the Book. II.
Montana Committee for the Humanities.
TX715.E1757 2005
641.59786--dc22
2005020394

Table of Contents ○○○○○○○○○○○○○○○○○○○○○○○○○○○○○○○○○○○○○

The Meat of the Story

All's Well That Ends Well

Foreword ○○

The Montana Committee for the Humanities and, to an even greater extent, our Montana Center for the Book and Montana Festival of the Book all do their good work through the generosity and support of our state's abundant writers and scholars. When Farcountry Press came to us with the idea of a Montana writers' cookbook, we seized upon it as a natural response to public interest, as yet another way to promote Montana's fine writing, and as a timely introduction to our *Key Ingredients: America by Food* exhibition from the Smithsonian Institution, which tours Montana from 2006 to 2007.

For their support of this project, we are grateful to the many writers from Montana and neighboring states who have shared with us their time, their recipes, and their writings about food. Kim Anderson at MCH and Caroline Patterson and Kelli Twichel at Farcountry Press have seen the project through from beginning to end, with the able research assistance of Pamala Burke and others. We are most grateful to Farcountry Press for its support of Montana writing and of our Montana Center for the Book.

Bon appétit et bonne lecture!

Mark A. Sherouse
Executive Director, Montana Committee for the Humanities

Introduction

I've heard many explanations for why Montana is as famous for its writers as it is for its scenery. First, of course, there's the scenery. There's space. People leave you alone if that's what you want. It's cheap (or at least it used to be). Winters are long. There's a tradition.

And there is, indeed, a tradition. From the legends and stories of the first Montanans to the most recent poems, novels, screenplays, and essays, we are a prolific bunch. Following the stories and songs of native peoples, the literature of frontier Montana begins with the *Journals of Lewis and Clark* and continues with the work of intrepid settlers and wanderers like Teddy Blue Abbot, Nanny Alderson, Andrew Garcia, and Granville Stuart. In the middle of the last century, voices as important and disparate as Mildred Walker, Joseph Kinsey Howard, A. B. Guthrie, Jr., and Dorothy Johnson both fed and corrected an increasingly romanticized vision of the West. More recent decades have seen yet another flourishing of important writing from Big Sky Country, including Mary Clearman Blew, Ivan Doig, Richard Ford, Jim Harrison, Richard Hugo, William Kittredge, Norman Maclean, Thomas McGuane, Wallace Stegner, James Welch, and many others.

But alongside the history, the romance, and the myth, there are some rougher realities about being a writer in Montana. It can be isolating, working so far from major cities and publishers. It's often hard to survive. It gets lonely. It gets cold.

Years ago, at a party during the Montana Festival of the Book, an editor from a major publishing house looked on in wonder as dozens of writers from across the state reunited with hoots and hugs and hollers. "If you got this many writers together in New York, there'd be blood on the floor within five minutes," he muttered. Most of the writers I've been lucky enough to know have been very good at "making their own fun," as my mother used to say. Especially when you work alone and inside your own head, when money is often an issue and the wind is howling at the door, the natural inclination out here is to have a party. Everyone comes, everyone talks, and everyone brings *something*. The stories, the laughter, the food, the drinks, somehow it all seems to come from the same place—a desire for community.

Here at the Montana Center for the Book, our job is to foster and tend that sense of community for both readers and writers. Through programs like the Montana Festival of the Book; our reading and discussion series, OpenBook; our annual invitation to all Montanans to read and discuss the same book, One Book Montana; and our reading and writing promotion program for young people, Letters About Literature; we try to celebrate, promote, and connect readers and writers. What makes the job thrilling is the enthusiasm that flows from both sides of the equation. Not only does Montana have great writers, it has great readers.

And we at the Montana Center for the Book have great friends: an advisory committee of citizens across the state who are involved in literary endeavors; the Montana Committee for the Humanities, our parent organization; and, most importantly, the writers. While we mailed recipe requests to the writers in our database, we may have overlooked some. If so, please contact us, as we are always striving to expand our listing of the area writers.

The writers in this book have shared—with each other, with their readers, and with the Montana Center for the Book—a tremendous amount over the years. Many of them have been featured at the Montana Festival of the Book, their works are part of our reading and discussion series; they teach; they contribute to conferences, panels, clubs, and service organizations; and they travel the state to promote literature and reading. These are generous folk. When they heard from me, yet again, asking for, of all things, recipes, they responded immediately. Just to help the cause, just to "make a little fun," just to pitch in.

This is big country. These are big hearts and big appetites. Enjoy.

Kim Anderson

Kim Anderson
Director, Montana Center for the Book

HIGH NOON

While savants debate the origin of the Martini, they're in agreement that America's trademark cocktail should only be made from gin. Of course, it's your privilege here in the Home of the Free to swill vodka or Everclear or even moonshine from that elegant Y-shaped glass and call it a Martini, but please don't try to pretend that you're a member of our club.

The first gin was distilled from the oil of juniper berries by a seventeenth-century Dutch professor of medicine named Franciscus de la Boe Sylvius, who was seeking a blood purifier. The Dutch word genever *was shortened by the English to gin, and, to my way of thinking, the best gin for a Martini is the elegant English spirit Bombay, chilled to zero degrees. The initial taste is sharp and glacial, like a stab wound from an icicle, and the "finish," as wine lovers say, hints of licorice, coriander, almonds, and, naturally, the fruit of junipers.*

4 ounces **Bombay gin,** chilled

Extra-dry **Martini & Rossi vermouth**

Martini shaker

1 **Connie's Tomato Chip**
(available at specialty food stores)

Serves 1.

1. First, put your bottle of Bombay overnight in the freezer compartment of your fridge. There's no danger that it will turn solid—most of these compartments are factory-set at zero, and Bombay will only begin to slush up at around 5 degrees below zero. Keeping the gin frigid subdues the raw bite of alcohol so that the sublime flavor of the drink shines through. And prohibiting the liquor from any contact with water or ice assures that this aristocrat won't be compromised by something, well, *common.*

2. Half an hour before Happy Hour put the glasses in the freezer, inverting them to discourage frost.

3. When the glasses are cold, pour the gin into a Martini shaker (or any clean, dry bottle), which has also been stored overnight in the freezer.

4. Depending on taste, spritz the bowls of the glasses with a few sprays of vermouth from a mister that has been chilled in the refrigerator (not the freezer—vermouth doesn't contain enough alcohol to resist freezing at that temperature). Some tough guys believe that a true dry Martini should only be *shown* the vermouth, but I think that's grandstanding. However, I always serve a small piece of chocolate before the drinks. Chocolate is the perfect warm-up act, and readies the palate for a totally opposite taste.

5. Shake the gin 'til it's frothy, pour immediately, and place in each glass a single Connie's Tomato Chip. These translucent confections, sliced ultrathin from organic heirloom tomatoes, are chewy and slightly acidic and mildly salted, another friend of the liquor. Swimming in the glass, a radiation of red and yellow, the little globe looks like the sun in a seamless sky, a promise of the warm and lazy hours to come.

A version of this article appeared in the "Blair Wine Project" in the April 2005 issue of *Outside*.

Moon Juice

If you thought Paul Giamatti's character in *Sideways* was obsessed, consider that for a growing number of American oenophiles, only wines made from ultra-organic "biodynamic" grapes will do.

Vintners producing this exalted fruit bury cow manure packed in cow horns at the moment of the fall equinox, unearth them on the vernal equinox, mix the contents with rainwater, and "dynamize" this muck by stirring it in alternate directions for an hour before spraying it on the soil. Other potions include flower heads of yarrow buried in stag's bladder, and oak bark composted in skull of goat. Cosmic and lunar cycles dictate when to harvest, when to "rack" new wine to remove the sediment, and even when to drink it.

One night I gathered some red wines for a raucous taste-test dinner that ended in slurpy talk. Compared to our as-advertised-on-television bottles, the biodynamic Frey 2002 Cabernet Sauvignon ($13) and the 2000 Pinot Noir and 2001 Cabernet Franc, from Robert Sinskey ($31 and $40), tasted more like the piquant little apricot I grew last summer. The real test was pitting these American wines against an aggressive American meal of cornbread, Monterey Jack cheese, and bison chili with New Mexico peppers. While the flavors of all three bottles stayed fresh and vibrant, the winner was Sinskey's Cabernet Franc, which was so full of nuances and dark secrets I went out into our forest after the last glass and bayed at the moon.

Bill Vaughn is the author of *First, a Little Chee-Chee, Then Some Other Extremely Odd Sports*. He is a contributing editor at *Outside*.

NEW YEAR'S DAY RAMOS FIZZ

First, excuses and disclaimers: I cannot in any actual way cook. I grew up in agriculture, a cookhouse culture, and never tried to transcend that limitation. A downtown café lay-about when on my own, I try to think of myself as a western traditionalist, deeply interested in good times and friends.

Question: How do you entertain at home when you can't cook?

Answer: Develop a specialty, like the New Year's Day Ramos Fizz

Tips: Make it clear that even invited guests are not welcome in your living room until four in the afternoon, three-thirty at the earliest. Persuade a deeply responsible person (preferably on the wagon) to take charge of the mixing. Your duties as host will render you less responsible as the evening proceeds into darkness. Provide the best you can afford.

Note: Make sure you have a blender, borrow if necessary.

○ ○

1 **egg,** separated
  (save egg yolks for later)

  Juice of half a **lemon**

½ teaspoon of **triple sec**

1 teaspoon of **powdered sugar**

1 teaspoon of **light cream**

2 ounces of **gin**
  (cheap is all right in this instance)

  Carbonated water

  Makes 1 portion, increase as necessary.

The Fizz Itself

1. The task of separating whites from yolks is demanding and onerous but must be faced, egg by damnable egg.

2. Put egg whites into blender and beat into soft peaks. Add rest of ingredients, blend, and shake over ice.

3. Pour several inches of the mix into a tall glass (try to think of this as approximately one portion, but let the guesswork begin). Fill rest of the glass with chilled carbonated water.

4. Make a sticky mess in the kitchen. Seize the evening. Tomorrow, and its idiot reckonings, is a long way off.

From "An Evening Out" in *Who Owns the West*, published by Mercury House, 1996.

Sliced apples and pears, various cheeses and decent wine: as evening came down over the old tree-lined boulevards on the north side of Great Falls, there was a well-lighted reception in the Charlie Russell Museum.

A raggedy man came in off the street, his shoes wrapped with silvery duct tape. Somebody told him the food and the drink were free. He smiled and poured for himself.

Somebody else wanted to show him out, but nobody did. I remember that fellow's judicious expression as he served himself a little plate of raw vegetables and dip and sipped his wine and studied a Russell painting, and the uneasiness in that hall full of the enfranchised (we the people with OK automobiles and new shirts). It is always healthy to be reminded that we are imposters (a little defeat is good for the liberal soul). The tension softened after somebody said the old man was probably the only person in the place Charlie Russell could have tolerated.

William Kittredge retired in 1997 after teaching creative writing at the University of Montana for 29 years. He has published a number of books, the latest of which is *The Best Stories of William Kittredge*, Graywolf Press, 2004.

13

GINGER PORTER

This recipe, which is adapted from Charlie Papazian's The New Complete Joy of Home Brewing, *makes a dark, snappy beer especially good for long winter evenings.*

○ ○

5 pounds **plain dark malt extract**
  (found in a home-brewing supply store)

$\frac{1}{4}$ pound **roasted barley**

1 pound **crystal malt**

$\frac{1}{4}$ pound **black patent**

1$\frac{1}{2}$ounces **Northern Brewer hops**
  (boiling)

1 cup **brown sugar**

1 cup **molasses**

2 inches **ginger root,** grated

6 ounces **unsweetened Baker's chocolate**

$\frac{1}{4}$ ounce **Willamette hops** *(finishing)*

1 ounce **ale yeast**

$\frac{3}{4}$ cup **corn sugar** *(for bottling)*

1 5-gallon **fermenter**

Makes 5 gallons.

1. Crush the grain malts and roasted barley.

2. Add them to $\frac{1}{2}$ gallon of cold water and heat.

3. When it starts to boil, remove the grains with a strainer.

4. Add the malt, black patent, hops, brown sugar, molasses, ginger, and chocolate. Boil for 45 minutes. Add the finishing hops for the final 2 minutes of boiling.

5. Sparge. (Isn't that a great word, *sparge*? For you non-home-brewers, it means to run through a strainer and rinse the dregs.)

6. In your fermenter, add cold water to the mixture to reach a total of 5 gallons. When it's cool, add the yeast.

7. Ferment a week, then add the bottling sugar. Bottle. I like to then wait at least 6 to 8 weeks before drinking.

**From "New and Noteworthy Books about the American West,"
a parody published in the *Denver Post* on April 1, 2002.**

Gretel Ehrlich,
The Solace of Open Cases.

In a bitterly cold winter, Wyomingites and their horses find meaning in multiple six-packs of Budweiser.

Larry McMurtry,
Lonesome Vulture.

One hundred and thirty years later, bankrupt Montana ranchers on horseback go on a big cattle drive to take their herds back to Texas.

John Nichols,
The Milagro Set Skirmishes.

Quaint, plucky Hispanic tenant farmers and their horses take on moneyed interests filming a Robert Redford movie.

John McPhee,
Encounters with the Archbrew-ed.

An ardent environmentalist, a dam-builder, a miner, and a real estate developer consider the merits of pilsners and stouts in a series of bull sessions on horseback at a trendy microbrewery.

A journalist, essayist, and business writer, **John Clayton** has lived in south-central Montana since 1990. *The Cowboy Girl*, his biography of the Montana/Wyoming journalist, novelist, and rancher Caroline Lockhart, will be published by the University of Nebraska Press in 2006.

John's essays and articles on the changing Rocky Mountain West have been featured in *High Country News*, *Montana Magazine*, the *Denver Post*, the *Seattle Times*, and dozens of other regional publications. He maintains a website and blog at www.johnclaytonbooks.com.

Robert Pack

4 or 5 **ice cubes**

1 jigger **gin** or **vodka**

Cold **tomato juice** or
V-8 vegetable juice

4 to 6 drops **Tabasco sauce**

½ jigger of **Worcestershire sauce**

Juice of half a **lemon** or **lime**

Optional: 1 teaspoon of
horseradish or **seasoned salt**

One **celery stick** or **olives**

Serves 1.

Robert Pack's newest collection, *Elk in Winter*, was published in 2004 by the University of Chicago, which also published *Rounding It Out, Minding the Sun* and *Fathering the Map: New and Selected Later Poems* in 1993. His most recent book of criticism, *Belief and Uncertainty in the Poetry of Robert Frost* was published in 2004.

BLOODY MARY

1. Put ice cubes in a tall glass and add gin or vodka.

2. Fill the glass almost to the top with cold tomato juice or V-8 vegetable juice.

3. Sprinkle in Tabasco sauce depending on how hot you like your drink.

4. Add Worcestershire sauce, according to preference.

5. Squeeze in lemon or lime juice.

6. Highly optional: Add horseradish.

7. Another option: Add seasoned salt.

8. Serve with celery stick and/or several olives.

9. Experiment to find exactly what suits your individual taste.

From "Maxims in Limbo," from *Walking to My Name*, published by John Hopkins Press in 1980 and used by permission.

In a time of joy
Eat bountifully;
In a time of sorrow
Also eat bountifully.

PEAR and FETA SALAD
with VINAIGRETTE DRESSING

1. In a small skillet, pour oil over minced shallots and heat until oil begins to sizzle. Reduce heat and simmer for 2 minutes. Remove from heat.

2. Whisk together port, vinegar, honey, and lemon juice. Whisk in hot oil and shallots. Dressing makes 3 cups—save the remaining dressing for your next salad.

3. Toss Romaine hearts and red onion with just enough dressing to coat the salad. Top with feta, pear slices, and pecans. Salt and pepper to taste. Serve immediately.

○ ○

Seckel Pear

O buttery sweetness, slope of musky pleasure,
The tongue's preoccupation. There's nothing
Like it in the world, nothing like its smoky shadow
Traveling the knotted branch. Nothing
Falls with such a slow-spiraled thud
Into the wet blades, or curves with such
Elegant promise among cow hooves
And crow feathers. Before the worm's advance,
Nothing glows with such sugary flesh or sleeps,
So intent and diligent, in its soundless bed.

Geraldine Connolly

The salad:

2 hearts of **Romaine lettuce,** chopped

$\frac{1}{4}$ cup of **feta cheese,** crumbled

1 ripe **pear,** sliced

1 small **red onion,** sliced

$\frac{1}{4}$ cup **pecans,** chopped

The dressing:

3 **shallots,** minced

2 cups **olive oil**

1 cup **port wine**

$\frac{1}{4}$ cup **balsamic vinegar**

2 tablespoons **honey**

2 tablespoons fresh **lemon juice**

Salad serves 4 to 6.

Geraldine Connolly is a poet and teacher who lives south of Bigfork, Montana, on the shores of Flathead Lake. She enjoys cooking with Montana delicacies such as morel mushrooms, black cherries, and antelope meat. Her books are *Food for the Winter*, published by Iris Press in 1998 and *Province of Fire*, published by Purdue University Press in 1990.

Salad Dressing

Bunch of **garlic bulbs**

Salt

Olive oil

Lemon juice

Makes enough dressing
for 2 salads.

Collards

Bunch of **collard greens,** washed

2 pieces **bacon,** chopped

2 tablespoons **onion,** chopped

Serves 3.

DARA'S SALAD DRESSING

From poet Dara Wier. Some people like the dressing so much they drink it (Bob Wrigley); others find it way too intense. Proportions are up to the chef.

1. Peel a bunch of garlic bulbs.

2. Mash them with salt until slimy, using a mortar and pestle.

3. Add olive oil and mash until mixed.

4. Squeeze in lemon juice and mash some more.

Use immediately. Toss over a salad of greens. Toss again with extra stuff, if feeling expansive: avocado, grapefruit, dried cherries, walnuts, red onion slivers . . . .

RICHARD'S COLLARDS

Richard Ford served this at Thanksgiving dinner at Jon Jackson and Jean Croxton's house. He brought the collards with him from New Orleans, just in case Montana was in short supply. Kristina dressed as a Pilgrim.

1. Remove spines from huge leaves and chop collards.

2. Cook up a couple of pieces of chopped bacon until crisp.

3. Add onion.

4. Turn heat up and toss in wet collards.

5. Stir constantly until collards are glossy with fat and are wilted.
You may serve at this point for extra-chewy collards; or cover, remove from heat, and let steam for a minute or two to soften.

"From Childhood," published in *Dangerous Neighborhoods*,
Cleveland University Press, 1994.

From Childhood

Weekend mornings we woke at dawn,

watched "Shock Theatre," sipped the dregs

of martinis, dragged butts. Our parents

slept late, hungover from the previous

nights' parties. Aliens, ghosts, homicidal

maniacs - nothing unsettled the headache quiet.

Marnie Prange was born
in Virginia, raised in North
Carolina, and attended the
University of Alabama in
Tuscaloosa. She is the
author of *Dangerous
Neighborhoods* and lives in
the Bitterroot Valley with
her husband, Greg Pape,
and their two sons,
Coleman and Clay.

KÖRÖZÖTT

Körözött is a Hungarian cheese spread that is the hors d'oeuvre of preference for my family, passed from grandmother to mother to two sisters and me, and now to our grown children. It is to be spread on crackers and accompanied, preferably, by a glass of wine, a gin and tonic, or whiskey on the rocks. For kids and teetotalers, any sparkling beverage will do.

○ ○

1 8-ounce package **cream cheese** *(whole or Neufchâtel light)*

1 stick **butter** *(or good margarine)*

3 to 5 *(depending on size)* **green onions,** chopped fine

1 shallow tablespoon **Hungarian paprika** *(more if you like a stronger flavor, but never hot paprika)*

1 teaspoon **caraway seeds**

½ teaspoon **Dijon mustard** *(optional)*

Dash of **salt** *(optional)*

Variations: Add **Tabasco sauce** or **anchovy paste,** to taste

Makes about 1½ cups.

1. Put cream cheese and butter in bowl at room temperature to soften.

2. Add chopped onions, paprika, caraway seeds, and, if you want, mustard and a dash of salt. Mix until spread is creamy and salmon pink. Chill.

3. Before serving, allow mixture to come to room temperature. Garnish with sprinkle of paprika.

4. The spread can be modified from this classic version. Occasionally, my mother added a bit of anchovy paste to the mix. I have sometimes added a few drops of Tabasco to pep up the taste buds.

From "Margitszitget Where It All Began" in *In This We Are Native*, published by Lyons Press in 2001.

Margaret Island rides plumb in the middle of the Danube, between the hills of Buda to the west and the sandy plain of Pest. It is a self-contained leafy world about a mile and a half long and five-hundred yards at its widest stretch. Great pools and springs of medicinal hot waters lie beneath the island's northern tip and along the river's shores. I knew little about the island or its ancient history, and as the van passed over the Arpad Bridge, I was jittery with anticipation. I only knew I was going to the park where, after they were married in Paris, my father took my mother on an August afternoon in 1932 to meet his family.

. . . On the lawns of the Grand Hotel, in the shade of giant chestnut and plane trees, the family broke bread at tables draped in white linens. They must have feasted on goose liver, salamis and ham, stuffed green peppers, cabbage, Dobos torte, and poppyseed cake. Perhaps the relatives toasted the new couple with champagne, but I like to imagine the lifted goblets of the ruby wine called *egri bkiaver* (bull's blood), which my father would, years later, order by the case for our own clan reunions.

Annick Smith is a freelance writer and filmmaker who lives in the Blackfoot valley of western Montana. Her parents and grandparents immigrated to Chicago from Hungary and Paris during the Great Depression.

With William Kittredge, she edited the Montana anthology *The Last Best Place*. She wrote *Homestead*, a memoir published by Milkweed Press in 1996, and *In This We Are Native*, essays about home, place, and travel, published by Lyons Press in 2001. She was executive producer of the feature film *Heartland* and co-producer of the film *A River Runs Through It*.

JUDY'S PARTY PENGUINS

These hors d'oeuvres sound more difficult than they are. By the time you make the third penguin, you'll be an expert. Trust me. They're adorable.

○○○

1 can of **jumbo pitted black olives**

1 8-ounce package **cream cheese,** softened

$\frac{1}{2}$ can of **small black olives**

1 large **carrot,** peeled

Frilly toothpicks in festive colors

Pastry bag, with #15 or #17 tip

Makes 18 penguins.

1. Bodies: Cut a slit from top to bottom, lengthwise, into the side of each jumbo olive. Using a pastry bag with a "ruffled" (#15 or #17) tip, insert about 1 teaspoon of cream cheese into each olive.

2. Feet: Slice the carrot into 18, $\frac{1}{4}$-inch-thick rounds; cut a small notch out of each carrot slice to form feet. Save the cut-out pieces.

3. Heads: Cut a small horizontal slit into the center of the small olive. Trim the "V" from a $\frac{1}{4}$- to $\frac{1}{16}$-inch thickness. Press the cut-out "V" of carrot into the slit to form the beak.

4. To assemble: Set a big olive, large hole side down, onto a carrot slice. Then, set a head onto the body, also large hole side down. Adjust so that the beak, cream cheese–ruffled chest, and notch in the carrot slice line up. Secure by pushing a frilly toothpick down through top of head until it sticks into the carrot feet. You should be able to pick each one up by its frilly "hat."

5. Arrange penguins in conversational groups on a nice plate. They also look great with a cheese ball igloo or an ice floe made of salmon pâté.

6. These can be made a few hours in advance. Drape the plate carefully with saran wrap to keep the olives from shriveling. Little spots of cream cheese on the plate will anchor their feet so the plate can travel without them tipping over.

From *Not Quite Stone*, published by the Merriam Frontier Award in 1992.

Thanksgiving Break

This time of year the leaves are squash and cranberry colors that run together no matter how you pile them. Tantalizing fogs roll down the sides of Sloway and Sentinel, snow whipped mounds I study like I study the mail on my doorstep, each line pulling me back to an earth and spice warm place where smooth whiskey and honey voices pool around the kitchen table and no one begs your pardon when elbows touch. This time of year, this far away the air bites deep and my courage rattles brittle as hollow bones, scared of any place too safe too easy to stay when my belly's full. It's time, I think, for a new custom. Time to roast a small pullet and lie in this bed like a mountain stream. Gone past the fork, casting free over rocks, me and Quartz Creek this fall are running, strong and clear.

Judy Blunt spent more than 30 years on wheat and cattle ranches in north-central Montana before leaving in 1986 to attend the University of Montana. Her poems and essays have appeared in numerous journals and anthologies. She is the recipient of a Jacob K. Javits Graduate Fellowship, a Montana Arts Council Individual Artist Fellowship, and, more recently, a 2004 National Endowment for the Arts Fellowship. Her memoir, *Breaking Clean*, published by Knopf in 2002, won the 1997 PEN/Jerard Fund Award, a 2001 Whiting Writers' Award, the 2003 Mountains and Plains Book Award, and the 2003 Willa Award for memoir/nonfiction. She is an assistant professor on the creative writing faculty of the University of Montana, Missoula.

23

RASPBERRY PEPPER JELLY

Pepper jelly was a family favorite during the ten years we lived in Tucson, Arizona. I created this recipe after moving to Montana, blending the taste of the Southwest with the raspberries that proliferate in our back yard in Helena. A few years ago, this ruby-red jelly won a blue ribbon at the Lewis and Clark County Fair. May Butler would have loved it!

3 to 4 pints of **raspberries,** depending on ripeness

$1\frac{1}{2}$ cups **cider vinegar**

4 **jalapeño peppers,** coarsely chopped

$5\frac{1}{2}$ cups **sugar**

$1\frac{3}{4}$ ounce box of **pectin**

1 teaspoon **butter**

Small **canning jars**

Makes 5 to 6 8-ounce jars

1. Crush and strain enough raspberries to make $2\frac{1}{2}$ cups of seedless juice.

2. To the strained juice, add cider vinegar and jalapeño peppers (more for hotter jelly). Bring the mixture to a boil, cool, and strain.

3. When the juice has cooled, add sugar, pectin, and butter. Stir well to disperse sugar and pectin as they tend to lump.

4. Bring to a rolling boil and continue boiling for 1 minute, stirring constantly. Pour jelly into prepared canning jars and seal.

5. Serve with cream cheese on crackers—its just as beautiful as it is delicious!

From "Profiles of the Century: May Butler," published in the *Helena Independent Record*, December 21, 1999.

Longtime Helena teacher May Butler was a large woman. Her house, high upon the hillside, was (and still is) accessible only by a series of steep stairs from the street. Every morning a taxi picked her up at the foot of the stairs and delivered her to school. Fortunately, May did not need to carry groceries and other packages up the stairs. Her father had long ago ingeniously constructed a slide leading from the rear alley above the house to the back door. The deliveryman pulled his vehicle into the alley and placed the items on the slide. With a gentle push they ended up nearly inside the kitchen.

Several octogenarians recalled with nostalgia that Miss Butler had been their teacher for first, second, and third grades. They remembered how her tiny hands and feet were a sharp contrast to her nearly three-hundred-pound frame. "But when you were little," one of the ladies declared, "and saw that hand coming at you, it looked huge!" Miss Butler was fond of whacking those who needed to be told more than once. And she kept an eye on the swings at recess, fearful that the smaller children might be hurt.

The former students agreed that Miss Butler was a formidable teacher, but she was also a lot of fun. Students often brought her presents from their mothers' kitchens. May was especially partial to homemade breads and jellies. She would cut the bread, open the jelly, lay it all out neatly on her desk, and invite everyone to have some. But she always added one condition, "Save the biggest piece for me!"

Ellen Baumler is the Montana Historical Society's interpretive historian. Her book, *Girl from the Gulches: The Story of Mary Ronan*, was published by the Montana Historical Society Press in 2003 and selected as a finalist award winner of the 2004 Willa Literary Awards. She was co-editor, with Dave Shors, of *Lost Places, Hidden Treasures*, published by the *Independent Record* in 2002. Ellen is well known for her Montana ghost stories, collected in two books, *Spirit Tailings* and *Beyond Spirit Tailings*, Montana Historical Society Press, 2002 and 2005, respectively.

2 **lobsters,** about 1½ pounds each

Kosher salt

3 tablespoons **olive oil**

2 **fennel bulbs,** top stalks, outer
layers removed, cut into small dice

1 **onion,** chopped

2 **garlic cloves,** chopped

3 medium **tomatoes,** quartered or
2 cups chopped, canned tomatoes

1 tablespoon **tomato paste**

1 cup **vermouth**

½ cup **Pernod**

1 cup fresh **orange juice**
(from 2 oranges)

2 teaspoons **dried tarragon**

Pinch of **pepper flakes**

Freshly ground **black pepper**

½ tablespoon **unsalted butter**

1 **orange,** skin and pith removed
and cut into sections

2 teaspoons **fresh tarragon,** chopped

REBECCA'S "My Hair is on Fire" LOBSTER SOUP

The Senator's office is aflame, my friends and I are having lunch with his senior policy advisor, Rebecca Manna, petitioning her and the Senator to support an economic development package for north Lincoln County that will include greater assistance for the last remaining roadless areas in the Yaak.

A poof and pop! of heated blue air soars past my nose, scorches my eyebrows, singes the top of my hair, then falls back to a wavering, wobbly orange flame that encases the leaking old Coleman stove, melting the counter in the Senator's conference room only a little.

The policy director's desk is piled high with thousands of papers and letters, all of the utmost urgency and importance—we recognize and appreciate the rarity of an audience with her—and we are determined to make the most of it, hence our offer to prepare lunch in her office, rather than traveling out somewhere, ordering cardboard pizza.

Is there a fire extinguisher? we ask. The smoke alarm begins to sound, lights flash, the building is evacuating. Does it really have to be this hard to get wilderness in the Yaak?

Lobster, Fennel, and Orange Soup

Cribbed from Gordon Hamersley and Joanne McAllister Smart's excellent Bistro Cooking at Home, with only slight variations. Gordon is a Yaak Valley Forest Council supporter; please patronize his wonderful restaurant, Hamersley's Bistro in Boston.

Gordon's Note: Serve this soup with some toasted baguette slices. Better yet, slather those baguette toasts with some garlicky aioli.

○ ○

The broth:

1. In a pot large enough for the lobsters, bring 6 quarts water to boil.

2. Add the lobsters and about a teaspoon of salt. Bring the water back to a boil and cook lobsters five minutes. Remove from the pot and let cool. Reserve 3 quarts of the lobster cooking water.

3. When lobsters are cool, remove meat from tails and claws, working over a bowl to collect the juices. Rinse the bodies under cold running water and reserve.

4. Heat the olive oil in a large soup pot over high heat. Put the lobster bodies in the pot and cook, stirring occasionally, for about 5 minutes. Reduce heat to medium-high and add half of the fennel as well as the onion, garlic, tomatoes, and tomato paste. Continue to cook, stirring, for another 10 minutes. The lobster shells will darken.

5. Add vermouth and Pernod to the pan. Bring to a boil over high heat, being alert to the chance that, like the director's hair, the Pernod can ignite. Let the Pernod boil away for a minute or two, stirring to scrape up any bits stuck to the pan. Add the reserved cooking water, orange juice, dried tarragon, and red pepper flakes. Also add any collected lobster liquid. Bring to a boil over high heat, lower to a simmer, and cook for 45 minutes.

6. Remove the lobster bodies from the pot—letting any excess liquid drain back into the broth—and discard. Strain the broth into a clean pot, pressing down on the solids to squeeze out liquid and flavor. Add salt and black pepper to taste. (This broth, which makes about 2 quarts, can be made a day ahead).

The soup:

1. Sauté butter in a small pan over medium-high heat until hot.

2. Add the remaining fennel and cook about 10 minutes.

3. Add the orange sections and fresh tarragon and remove from the heat.

4. Add cut-up lobster meat.

5. Add hot lobster broth and cook over medium heat for a few minutes before serving.

Rick Bass is the author of 21 books (at last count) including his newest, *The Diezmo*, as well as *Caribou Rising: Defending the Porcupine Herd, Gwich-'In Culture, and the Arctic National Wildlife Refuge; The Hermit's Story; Colter: The True Story of the Best Dog I Ever Had;* and *The Ninemile Wolves.* He lives in the Yaak with his wife and two daughters.

The Senator and his staff have been good to the residents of Lincoln County, but we are seeking a hero, a champion for the Yaak. Somewhere along the line we have gotten it into our minds that if we could only cook the perfect meal, the Senator's heart would open further to understand more clearly the depths of our love for these last roadless lands, and that the Senator could then understand the incredible moderation of our asking for the last of the last, in a land where not one single acre of wilderness has been designated north of the Kootenai River.

Rick Bass

In meeting after meeting, and nurturing, in the most literal sense, our champion, we put forth our best efforts, trying to articulate the beauty of our beloved wildlands: the Northwest Peaks, Roderick and Grizzly and Pink mountains, Mount Henry, the West Fork, Buckhorn Ridge, and all our other little gardens of wildness: all beloved, and all rare.

The language of wilderness in the Yaak—of wilderness-to-come—is that of loon, willow, black bear, wolverine, grizzly, feldspar, glacier, lupine. The language of our crude articulation, our cuisine and cookery, contains phrases like "clarify the butter" and "prepare a mirepoix" and "assemble the bouquet garni."

The language of our time spent in the Senator's office contains phrases like "Walk me around the mulberry bush" and "At the end of the day...." We speak of putting the ball across the goal line, and of the need for collaboration, and yet of the need also for sharp elbows.

So many dialects, so many tongues! Maybe we are not so crazed after all to think that one perfect dish can still, even now, bring together all participants into one focused moment of mutual understanding in which the clarity of a solution is attained. Somehow, we have gotten it into our minds that the solution, wilderness in the Yaak, will be as permanent and enduring as is the pleasure of the palate fading even in the moment, temporal and fleeting. We believe it.

The best meal of all? A piece of French bread and thick yellow cheese and a canteen of cold well-water, on top of a nameless ridge in the Yaak, looking down into the uncut basin below, in the autumn, with forests of larch stretching unbroken to the horizon. But in the meantime, this recipe, from the day Rebecca's office caught on fire.

Please send your letters for Yaak wilderness to Yaak Valley Forest Council, 155 Riverview, Troy, Montana 59935 or info@yaakvalley.org.

WATERCRESS SOUP

Years ago, one of my "rites of spring" was making watercress soup. Near a warm spring, I had a favorite spot to find watercress, and, after washing it carefully with just a drop or two of bleach and then rinsing it a number of times in clear water, I proceeded to make the soup. One year, I decided to dry some watercress so that I could make the soup any time of the year. (These days it can be found in the supermarket.) With the dried watercress I can serve a hot cup of soup as part of the cocktail hour before a winter dinner party.

2 bunches **watercress**

2 thick slices **onion**

1 3-inch piece of **celery,** cut up

1 tablespoon **cornstarch**

1 tablespoon **sugar**

1 teaspoon **salt**

3 cups **chicken bouillon**

1 large can **evaporated milk**

2 tablespoons **butter**

Serves 5 to 6.

1. Remove stems from watercress leaves and discard.

2. Place watercress leaves, onion, celery, cornstarch, sugar, salt, and 2 cups of chicken bouillon in blender and blend until smooth.

3. Place in saucepan and add remaining 1 cup of bouillon. Bring mixture to a boil; reduce heat and cook for 10 minutes, stirring constantly.

4. Add evaporated milk and butter and simmer for 5 minutes. Garnish with a bit of fresh watercress.

From *Grace Stone Coates: Her Life in Letters*, published by Riverbend Publishing in 2004.

And then there is food for the soul...

When asked if he understood Grace, Henderson would say, 'Hell, no, I don't understand her. I just love her.' He indulged her, but did not understand her compulsion to write. Nor did he understand her need to feed the soul and mind as well as the body. The first thing she would do in the morning, even before dressing, would be to grab a book and read a paragraph or verse.

Lee Rostad's most recent work is *Grace Stone Coates: Her Life in Letters*, a biography of a Montana writer in White Sulphur Springs who regularly corresponded with William Saroyan, H. G. Merriam, and Frank Bird Linderman. Rostad's other publications include *Fourteen Cents & Seven Green Apples: The Life and Times of Charles Bair* and *Grace Stone Coates: Honey Wine and Hunger Root.* She is a member of the Montana Historical Society board of directors, a former member of the Montana Committee for the Humanities, and a recipient of the Montana Governor's Humanities Award.

Leonard Schonberg

The soup:

1 pound firm **fish filet**
(cod or flounder)

Kosher salt

3 tablespoons **olive oil**

1 large **onion,** chopped

2 cloves of **garlic,** minced

1 tablespoon grated **orange zest**

The stock:

2 14-ounce cans of **99% fat free chicken soup**

1 8-ounce bottle of **clam juice**

$\frac{1}{3}$ cup of **orange juice**

2 tablespoons **fresh lime juice**

Salt and **pepper** to taste

Chopped **fresh mint** or **parsley** as garnish

Serves 3 to 4.

SPANISH FISH SOUP with ORANGE

1. Cut the fish into strips, $\frac{1}{2}$-inch wide and $1\frac{1}{2}$-inches long. Sprinkle with kosher salt.

2. In a small saucepan over medium heat, warm the oil. Sauté onion and garlic until tender and translucent, then reduce heat to low, but don't allow onion to color. Add the orange zest and stir well, pour in the stock, and simmer for 15 minutes.

3. Add the fish pieces and cook until tender (7 to 10 minutes).

4. Stir in the orange juice and lime juice, season with salt and pepper, and serve. Garnish with mint or parsley.

○○○

From *Morgan's War*, published by Sunstone Press in April 2005.

Robert left a message at the Medecins sans Frontieres office for Jean to call him at the hospital. On a Wednesday evening, he met Jean and Simone outside an Afghan restaurant near Shoiba Bazaar. The Pakistanis and Afghans passing turned to look at them, even though Simone had her head covered. The restaurants' patrons, all men, stared at them as they entered. Those with their backs to the door swung around in their chairs. An Afghan waiter materialized as soon as they passed the threshold, looked nervously from Simone to the men inside, then led them to a dark stairwell, where they climbed to a room on the upper floor. Its sole occupant was a sheep. A young man in a soiled salwar kameez stained with old blood poked his head in the door. The waiter snapped at him brusquely in Pashto and he tied a rope around the sheep's neck. He dragged it from the room, returning moments later with a piece of cardboard to sweep the sheep droppings from the floor into a small pile just outside the doorway. The waiter in the meantime carried in a low table and cushions. When they were all seated on the cushions around the table, their knees crossed uncomfortably under them, he asked them if they wanted tea or soda, then disappeared from the room.

"In English, you would say quaint, no?" Jean said, smiling.

"Very."

Jean stepped onto the open wooden balcony outside the window and called to Simone and Robert to join him. It was already dark, the last vestiges of light no more than pale blue and purple streaks just above the western horizon. They peered down into the crowded street and saw the young man who'd cleaned their room placing cuts of lamb on a grill almost four feet long. The hot charcoal flared into orange and red flames as fat dripped onto it.

The waiter reappeared with their drinks and they sat down again. He handed each of them a slab of naan, a flat bread that would serve as their plate, and a cloth napkin, more gray than white. The smell of grilled lamb drifted through the window, making them all hungry.

"We've eaten here once before," Simone said. "The customers downstairs had the same reaction. They are not accustomed to having a woman in the restaurant. The food is delicious in spite of how—" she grasped for the word. "Primitive. Yes, that is the word."

Leonard Schonberg is an author, physician, and actor. His four novels, *Deadly Indian Summer*, *Fish Heads*, *Legacy*, and *Morgan's War*, have been published by Sunstone Press of Santa Fe, New Mexico. As an actor, he has appeared on stage and in television soap operas. He lives on a ranch in the Elkhorn Mountains of Montana.

2 tablespoons **onion,** coarsely chopped

1 clove **garlic,** minced

1 tablespoon **butter, margarine,** or **oil**

1 cup **carrots,** diced

$\frac{1}{2}$ cup **celery,** diced

$\frac{1}{2}$ cup **mushrooms,** finely chopped

$1\frac{1}{2}$ tablespoons **flour**

6 to 7 cups homemade **chicken** or **turkey stock**

1 teaspoon **marjoram**

Salt and **pepper** to taste

1 cup **alphabet pasta**

1 cup cooked **chicken** or **turkey,** diced,

Dash **hot pepper sauce** to taste

2 tablespoons **parsley,** chopped

Serves 5 to 6.

ABECADARIAN SOUP

1. In a large saucepan, sauté the onion and garlic in butter until soft.

2. Add the carrots, celery, and mushrooms and cook the vegetables, stirring them, 3 to 5 minutes.

3. Add flour and cook, stirring all the while, for another minute.

4. Add the stock, marjoram, salt, and pepper. Bring the soup to a boil. Reduce the heat, partially cover the pan, and simmer the soup for about 1 hour.

5. Add the pasta, chicken, and hot pepper sauce. Adjust the seasonings and heat the soup to boiling.

6. Sprinkle the soup with parsley just before serving.

From *The Bookstore Mouse*, published by Harcourt Publishers in 1995.

In this scene, Cervantes, the bookstore mouse, prepares his supper.

There were lots of recipes to choose from, because I ate my meals out of a thick cookbook. Before it had fallen down from the cooking section, three shelves above, I was limited to the few tasty words I could find scattered in my dictionary. But with the cookbook, all I had to do was tear out the list of ingredients and mix the words together. Then I could enjoy such delicacies as *Mexican Rice* or *Cajun Chicken*.

That day I had a hard time deciding what to eat. *Barbequed Ribs?* No, they sounded a bit sticky. *Hawaiian Pork Chops?* Too exotic. I'd never come across Hawaiian before and I didn't want to take a chance. But then I found it. *Roast Pork with Herbs.* Anything with the word herbs in it was bound to be good; they added such flavor to a meal. After I had chosen my entrée, I slowly carved the paper with my nail, care-ful to slice through only the top layer. If I cut too deep, I would lose the recipe on the back of the page. But the paper in this cookbook was thick and of good quality, and it was easy for me to peel off the words.

With all the ingredients assembled, I wadded them up and popped the succulent morsel into my mouth.

I rolled the words around on my tongue…*rosemary, oregano, thyme, sage*…oh, they were so delicious!

Peggy Christian is a children's author whose books include: *If You Find a Rock*, published by Harcourt Publishers in 2000, an imaginative exploration of the kinds of rocks we find every day, as well as *Chocolate the Glacier Grizzly Bear*, published by Benefactory Press in 1997, the true story of the successful relocation of a young grizzly bear in Glacier National Park. For older readers, she wrote *The Old Coot*, published by Atheneum in 1992, a collection of original fables of the Old West, and *The Bookstore Mouse*, a fantasy about reading and the dangers of censorship. She has written articles for magazines and journals and is at work on an adult book of essays on the reading life.

Peggy has a graduate degree in linguistics from the University of Montana and teaches writing to students of all ages. She volunteers for a number of literacy organizations and in her spare time does creative bookbinding. She lives in Missoula with her husband, and has two college-aged sons who love to read.

2 **red onions,** chopped in $\frac{1}{2}$-inch dice

2 ounces **olive oil**

1 cup **red wine**

$\frac{1}{2}$ cup **red wine vinegar**

20 ripe **peaches,** pitted and quartered

$\frac{1}{4}$ cup **brown sugar**

$\frac{1}{2}$ teaspoon **red pepper flakes**

2 teaspoons **mustard seeds**

1 **cinnamon stick**

Serves approximately 8.

PETER HOFFMAN'S PEACH CHUTNEY

1. In a medium saucepot, cook the onions in olive oil until lightly browned.

2. Add the wine and vinegar and bring to a boil.

3. Add the peaches, spices, and sugar. Turn off the heat and steep for 15 minutes.

4. Cool; season with salt and pepper to taste.

This is a wonderful accompaniment to roast pork.

From "Live to Ride: The Dedicated Bikers' Dream," published in the March 1999 issue of *Outside*.

Three times a week, Peter Hoffman pedals from his brownstone in Manhattan's Chelsea neighborhood to the Union Square farmer's market, where he picks up a couple hundred pounds of whatever looks good and cycles it all down to SoHo, to his chic Mediterranean-influenced restaurant, Savoy. His bike's central cargo hold is also how he rickshaws his five-year-old to kindergarten, and how he shuttles wine from home to work. Usually the system works just fine. "But I did once dump a case of California cabernet in an intersection," admits the 42-year-old chef.

He rides year-round, in all weather, his payload the ripest fruits and veggies of the moment: Hoffman tailors Savoy's menu to what's in season, what's regionally grown, and of course, what's schleppable. His last find, a load of "superb" quinces that became chutney for grilled veal, nearly wiped out his legs. "Fall's the killer," he says, "all those apples and pumpkins and parsnips."

His rig is a Long Haul, custom-made in Oregon by Jan VanderTuin of Eugene's Human Powered Machines and built by at-risk school kids. Inspired by a 1920s Danish design, VanderTuin stretched the wheelbase to 73 inches and added a powerful spring-activated double-sided kickstand, drum brakes, and 21 gears. Hoffman had VanderTuin base the dimensions of the custom cargo bin on a crate of apples and the plastic containers used for shipping fragile greens. The carrier is fabric-lined, so his whole family can get cozy in the hold.

Florence Williams is a contributing writer for *Outside* magazine. Her articles and essays also appear in the *New York Times, the New Republic, High Country News,* and other publications. She received an MFA in creative writing at the University of Montana in 1994 and lives with her family in Helena.

GRZYBI (Mushrooms)

This recipe was brought from Poland by my grandmother, Anna Laskowski, who passed it on to my mother, Clare Dylewski Laskowski. It is my favorite side dish next to the turkey and stuffing during the winter holiday season.

○ ○

16 ounces of fresh **mushrooms**
(or if you have the knowledge my grandmother had, you can go pick your own)

1 large **onion**

2-inch square of **salt pork**

2 to 3 tablespoons of **cream**

$\frac{1}{2}$ to 1 tablespoon of **flour**

Pepper according to taste

Serves 4.

1. Slice mushrooms and onions and rinse.

2. In a medium-sized pot, cover mushrooms and onions with water and boil on low for half an hour.

3. Dice salt pork into very small pieces. Fry salt pork until golden, not crisp.

4. Add salt pork and drippings to the onions and mushrooms.

5. In a separate bowl, mix cream with flour to make a flour paste. Slowly and gradually pour flour paste into the mushroom mixture till thickened.

6. Add pepper according to taste. Do not use salt.

○ ○

From *Every Good Boy Does Fine*, published by Southern Methodist University Press in 2003.

On Monday I pretend to be ill. I complain long and loud enough that the group home staff relent and let me stay home. Lorna again feels good enough to be out of her room, even to be wheeled to the backyard where staff and residents have begun planting peas and cucumbers, carrots and onions.

The morning sun haloes her head, and she smiles. I say hello, but I don't think she hears; she is in another place right now. After a silence, she turns her head, looks surprised to see me there.

"Robert, I had a garden, definitely," she says. "I have two girls and a boy. Have I ever shown you their pictures? They're such beautiful kids. And my house, have you ever seen my house? Tucked away in the woods with a redwood deck and young cedar tress guarding the back. We had lots of deer, and I saw a mountain lion once. I kept the kids inside for a week after that, till I heard they shot a lion down the road a little ways. Do you remember, Robert?"

"Sure," I say.

Lorna raises a shaky empty hand to her mouth as though trying to feed herself. I grab a plastic bottle with a straw from a picnic table and hold it near her mouth. She sucks but then coughs and spits out the thickened formula. I put the bottle down and hold her hand.

"What do you think, Robert? Are we lucky to be here now? Such a beautiful day. I think I smell lilacs."

"Yes, Lorna," I say, and can't think of anything else though I feel there's a lot more that could be said.

"Nothing hurts this moment," she says. "If I sit just like this and think good thoughts."

"See, Lorna, you're getting better. Tomorrow we'll go out. We'll celebrate."

"I'm exhausted," Lorna says. "Definitely. It's been a long day."

"It's only morning," I begin to tell her, but she dips her chin, her eyes close, her breathing becomes regular and deep and, like that, she is asleep.

She is asleep for a long time. On Tuesday, nurses come and attach tubes. She will be fed by tube, medicated by tube. Her face is contorted. She doesn't speak more than a word at a time. I sit by her into the night and try to pray.

Tim Laskowski wrote *Every Good Boy Does Fine* and is coauthor of *A Race to Nowhere: An Arms Race Primer for Catholics.* His fiction, poetry, essays, and reviews have appeared in many literary venues. The grandson of Polish immigrants, Laskowski grew up in Erie, Pennsylvania. He earned his BA in social work from Gannon University; an MA in English and MFA in creative writing from the University of Montana; and a PhD from Ohio University. Laskowski works for Community Medical Center in Missoula as a case manager for people with physical disabilities and has a 16-year-old son, Evan. He currently lives in Lolo with his fiancée, Angelika Mitchell.

MANGO SALSA for GRILLED WILD SALMON

3 large ripe **mangos,** peeled and chunked

½ cup **red onion,** finely chopped

Half (or whole, depending on taste) of a **Serrano pepper,** minced

1½ tablespoons **fresh ginger root,** minced

¼ cup **olive oil**

Juice of half a **lime**

1 tablespoon **Nambe chili powder,** not for heat but flavor *(available at any specialty store)*

10 **tomatillos,** husks removed, blanched for 15 seconds, towel-dried and chopped

2 tablespoons **turbinado sugar**

1 bunch fresh **cilantro,** stemmed and coarsely chopped

Serves 6.

1. Two to three hours before dinner, in a crockery bowl combine prepared mangos, onion, Serrano pepper, ginger root, olive oil, lime, and chili powder. Refrigerate.

2. In a second bowl, toss prepared tomatillos with sugar. Cover.

3. Half an hour before dinner, allow mango mixture to come to room temperature. Combine contents of bowls and, just before serving, add cilantro.

4. Toss and spoon across grilled wild salmon.

Leftover salsa makes an elegant salad dressing for sliced avocado on a bed of greens—just add more olive oil, chili powder, sugar, and lime to taste.

From "Take Me, Take My Flies" in *Barefoot Hearted: A Wild Life Among Wildlife*, published by Villard Press in 2001.

I'm living in a seventy-five-year-old barn not quite made habitable for humans, with a mate who's cavalierly oblivious to insect life. More pinched than usual, we are awaiting my fall royalty check to order the season's supply of Fly Scoops: oblong white plastic holders, lined with sticky paper, designed to fasten on windows. Note: The species Pollenia rudis, the cluster fly, is larger and blacker than a housefly, but, thankfully, not of the grouping "filth flies."

Before plunging into dinner preparation, I had busted flies off the windows for half an hour, two hundred or more, yet with such a reluctance for the chore—sorely missing my scoops—I hadn't captured the lot. Now with the windows growing dark, flies homed for the electric lights. I set out the makings for salsa—tomatoes, red onion, jalapeño pepper, fresh cilantro—and began to wield the chopping blade. I opened two cans of black beans, gave them a good rinsing, and dumped them with a cup of water into a small pot and set it on a back burner. *Thwap-thwap-thwap.* Above the stove, four fat-bellied flies rebounded inside the aluminum shade of a reflector lamp. Black beans and flies, I had well learned, are quite indistinguishable lumped together. I dropped a tight-fitting lid on the pot. To the salsa, I next added cumin, cayenne, a shot of olive oil, a good squeeze of lime. All the while I worked, I kept my sights trained like search beams, scanning the countertops and floor. Into each of two heating cast-iron skillets, I slid a corn tortilla topped with a stout slice of Swiss cheese, and I plunked on the lids—mostly, this time, to seal in the heat to melt the cheese, the idea being to soften it into a shiny, gooey pool without crisping or browning the tortilla, or bubbling the cheese. It's a technique that requires, midway through the melting, slipping a second tortilla under the first.

On the dining table, I arranged the bowl of salsa along with smaller dishes of sliced avocado, black olives, strips of red lettuce, and Nancy's yogurt. Half a dozen flies, attracted to the milky plastic dome-of-a-chandelier overhead, caromed around with the zing of pool balls from a hard-hit opening break. Cluster flies, for their final hour of life, pour on the speed then plummet like aerial battery toys run out of juice. Ten or twelve more clung nearby to the ceiling beams, just waiting their turns. I swept the bowls to a corner of the table, out of range of falling bodies. Back in the kitchen, four corpses screamed to be plucked off the floor. Another three, half-expired, sprawled beneath the dish drainer—two helplessly on their backs, legs jiggling in final spasms, the third splayed nose-down in a splash of water. I snatched up the toilet paper roll (we were clean out of tissues, too pricey for

this month's budget), ripped off three squares, scooped up the seven blackguards, and fired them into the garbage.

Patrick, at that moment, walked in and sat down at the table, his usual reading spot, and picked his Anvil magazine out of the pile of mail. "Anything I can do?" he asked.

Seeing him thus positioned and with such an offer, I was momentarily heartened. "Oh good!" I said. "You can be on fly patrol."

"Oh, I'll be on tight fly patrol," he avowed.

Tricked, again.

"Yeah, I'll bet!" The words escaped, half under my breath. With a big slotted spoon, I flung a portion of black beans—imagining them all turned to flies—on top of his tortillas and cheese. I slung the plate down in front of him and sang, "Here's a lovely fly taco, my sweet!" Fetching my own plate, I settled across from him and slid the bowls of fixings to the middle of the table. At which, I noticed a large fly landing on my dearest. "There's a big fat bugger on your shoulder." I pointed.

Patrick's head slowly swiveled. He looked the insect in the eye—some bit of brotherhood flashed between them, I swear—then he swiveled back, his gaze locking tight on me. "Pretend it's a parrot."

Kathleen Meyer wrote *How to Shit in the Woods: An Environmentally Sound Approach to a Lost Art, Barefoot Hearted: A Wild Life Among Wildlife*, and the upcoming *Toiletopia: The Life and Ludicrous Times of an Unlikely Best-selling Author*, due out in early 2006. She lives in the central Bitterroot Valley; visit her at www.KathleenintheWoods.com

SPOON BREAD

My family is from Texas, as was much of the cooking I grew up with. Cornmeal worked its way into many things: corn sticks, cornbread dipped in buttermilk, the coating for fried chicken and fried tomatoes, the stuffing for turkey at Thanksgiving. Spoon bread is some-place between cornbread and pudding, and it tastes best eaten with a bit of additional butter melting on top.

2 cups **yellow cornmeal**

$\frac{3}{4}$ teaspoon **salt**

2 tablespoons **butter**

1 cup boiling **water**

2 **eggs,** separated into yolks and whites

2 teaspoons **baking powder**

$1\frac{1}{2}$ cups **milk**

Serves 6.

1. Place corn meal, salt, and butter in a mixing bowl and pour in boiling water while stir-ring constantly. Set aside until cool.

2. Beat egg whites until stiff. Set aside.

3. Lightly beat egg yolks and along with baking powder and milk, add to cooled corn-meal mixture. Blend well.

4. Fold in beaten egg whites.

5. Pour into greased baking dish. Bake in 350° oven for 45 minutes.

From *Hitch*, published by Harcourt Children's Books in 2005.

In this scene, several Civilian Conservation Corps enrollees at the Fort Missoula conditioning camp encounter CCC food for the first time.

Reese led my group to some tables in one corner, and as soon as we sat down other CCC'ers began bringing us food: pitchers of milk; vast platters of meat loaf and sliced bread; bowls of green beans, mashed potatoes, gravy; dishes with butter and jam. Talk rose at other tables, jokes and laughter, but we sat in stunned silence.

So much food!

A thin guy seated opposite me wore an expression like he couldn't believe what he was seeing. "Holy moley! I didn't know anybody ate like this outside of the movies."

"You don't need permission to eat," Reese said. "Serve yourselves some of whatever's in front of you and pass it along."

The thin guy carefully put a small spoonful of potatoes on his plate and then, with a quick glance like he was afraid somebody would stop him, took a second, larger serving. And then up and down the table, others were doing the same thing. In minutes every one of us enrollees was digging into a plateful of food.

Jeanette Ingold began her writing career on the staff of the *Missoulian*. Her short stories and half a dozen novels are on recommended reading lists in numerous states. *The Window* was an American Library Association Best Book for Young Adults and an International Reading Association Young Adults' Choice. *Airfield* and *Pictures, 1918*, were selected as New York Public Library Books for the Teen Age. *The Big Burn* won the Western Writers of America Spur Award for Juvenile Fiction. Her newest books bring her writing home to Montana: *Mountain Solo*, an excursion into the Rattlesnake Wilderness outside Missoula, and *Hitch*, the story of a young man's experiences in a Civilian Conservation Corps camp.

SALARETUS BISCUITS

In the mid-1860s, the measure of a woman's worth was taken by the quality of the biscuit and the crust of the pie she set on her table.

○○

4 parts **flour**

1 tablespoon **soda**
    for each quart of flour

   Salt, to taste *(about ¼ teaspoon)*

2 parts **lard, butter,** or
    combination of both

1 part **buttermilk** or **milk**

1. Toss sifted flour, soda, and salt into a bowl.

2. Divide the shortening into two parts. Take half the shortening and cut into flour with fingers, 2 knives, or a pastry cutter, until the mix feels mealy. (This is what makes the biscuit short or "tender.") Add rest of shortening and work until pea-sized. (This is what gives the biscuit its flake).

3. Add buttermilk or milk and mix with fork until it forms a ball.

4. Pat the round of dough into a ½-inch-thick slab and pat into a large square. Cut into 2-inch squares and place on greased cookie sheets with at least an inch between each.

5. Bake at 450° for 15 to 20 minutes. If you're using a wood stove, the right temperature has been reached when a tablespoon of flour scorches within 10 minutes of being tossed on the oven floor.

From *Strength of Stone: the Journal of Electa Bryan Plumer, 1862-1864*, published by Globe Pequot, Two Dot Imprint, in 2002.

October 19, 1862. He's back! Thank God. He's back. And he's brought with him two competent riflemen and put them up in one of the Indian "houses." So much to record, I hardly know where to begin. Swift was filling the water barrels when he saw them coming. He threw open the gates yelling, "They're here! They're here!" And we all ran out to meet them. Mr. Vail rode in first on the govt. farm's little dun Indian pony and close behind came a man on a big buckskin. Last, William Henry Handy Plumer, astride a dancing bay mare he calls Lady Mac, short for MacBeth because, he says, she's so high strung she'll be the death of him. I don't believe it. He rides so one with his mount, he puts the agile Indian to shame. Besides the bay, he led a fine sorrel packed with his belongings.

[Would you believe, Mr. Vail brought for us a good-sized sack of dried apples and a couple of hanks of yarn? How on earth did he ever get a hold of yarn, we wondered? Turns out, one of the Benton traders, thinking some woman new to the territory might be wanting such, brought it up from St. Louis. Indeed he thought rightly. He brought to each of the children a piece of colorful hard candy. Didn't they think that was a treat? They haven't seen likes of it since we left the Emilie.]

At supper we had so much to thank our Lord for that our food was nearly in danger of cooling before we were ready to eat. We served a fresh haunch of the venison and the ducks with potatoes, squash, fresh corn, salaretus biscuits, sweet buttermilk, and of course, one of my mince pies. To hear the men talk, one would have thought years had passed since they'd eaten a good meal. Even Bixby made some audible affirmation. Would you believe?

In 2002 **Diane Elliott's** novel *Strength of Stone: The Journal of Electa Bryan Plumer, 1862-1864*, was short-listed for the William Saroyan International Prize for Literature and garnered the Willa silver award in historical fiction. Ms. Elliott's poetry, short stories, and short shorts have appeared in such literary magazines as *Negative Capability, Yokoi, Montana Art Paper, Korone, and The Writer's Bar-B-Q.* She has received awards from the Montana Institute of the Arts, the National Writers Club, and the Mary Brennen Clapp Memorial Poetry Competition. In response to a commission from the Montana Ballet Company, she wrote *Impersonating Bernie*, based on her poetic novel *Songs of Bernie Bjorn*, which was produced in 1993. When she's not writing from her retreat in the old Pony jail in the Tobacco Root Mountains, she lives in Bozeman with her husband and Jack Russell terrier, Annie.

43

In a large bowl, combine:

1 cup **blue cornmeal** *(my favorite, but yellow or white is good)*

$\frac{1}{2}$ cup all-purpose **white flour**

$\frac{1}{2}$ cup **soy flour**

1 teaspoon **baking soda**

1 teaspoon **baking powder**

1 teaspoon **salt** *(or less, to taste)*

In a smaller bowl, mix:

$1\frac{1}{2}$ cups **unsweetened soy milk**

2 **eggs,** beaten lightly into the soy milk

1 cup grated **cheese** or grated soy "cheese" *(cheddar and/or Monterey Jack or Pepper Jack will taste better, but soy cheese is not at all bad)*

Note: this ingredient needn't sit soaking in the milk and egg mixture; add before combining all the ingredients below.

In a medium skillet, sauté:

1 tablespoon **shortening**

$\frac{1}{2}$ cup **yellow onion,** chopped well

3 or 4 **garlic cloves,** finely chopped

4 or more **chile peppers,** chopped—a couple of jalapeños, Serranos, yellow wax or red Fresnos, for example

Makes 6 pieces.

LOW-CARB, LOW-CAL CORNBREAD

This began as an experimental variation on my basic cornbread, in an attempt to reduce the high carbohydrate and caloric content. In short, if I wasn't able to come up with something palatable, I probably wouldn't be eating any more cornbread. But to my satisfaction this bread turned out to be very tasty indeed, and it is quite low in carbs and calories, as well as high in protein.

1. Preheat oven to 425°. Heat 2 tablespoons of shortening in an 8-inch black iron skillet in oven.

2. Remove the hot skillet from the oven and allow it to cool a bit while you combine the dry ingredients and the milk and eggs mixture.

3. Add in the cooled extra shortening mixture. Mix all the ingredients by hand thoroughly without beating.

4. Pour into the still-warm skillet and place into the oven. At my altitude, approximately 4,000 feet, it will take at least 50 minutes to bake. But check on it at 40 minutes and let it go as long as an hour, until it gets that very brown crust, or when it moves easily in the pan if you shake it (bear in mind that if your skillet is not well seasoned it may not move at all, so don't rely too heavily on this test). Check for doneness with a toothpick— the toothpick should come out more or less clean.

The result will be a rather nutty, somewhat tangy cornbread, quite suitable for buttering and eating with honey or molasses, or whatever. If you feel a need for sugar, add some, or some Splenda. Sweetness is not a characteristic of Southern cornbread. My mother always said it was "a Yankee notion," wrinkling her nose in distaste. And I must say, if the cornbread is to be eaten hot with butter and honey, why on earth would one add sugar?

From *Grootka*, published by Countryman Press in 1990.

Mulheisen opened the wine while Meldrim rinsed and dried the fish on paper towels. "I cleaned these fish this morning," he explained. He mixed flour, corn meal and a few dried herbs in a shallow dish and dredged the fish in it.

He asked Mulheisen to chop up a small onion. He put a large, black-iron skillet on the electric range and spooned in three large tablespoons of brownish fat from a jar he'd taken from the refrigerator. "Bacon fat," he explained. "I prefer it for pan-fried fish. Some would say it has too much flavor for these sweet little bluegills, but I like it...."

Meldrim gently lowered the fish into the hot bacon fat. They sizzled while he shook up a mixture of olive oil and wine vinegar, along with selected herbs, in a glass cruet and handed it to Mulheisen along with the salad to be placed on the bar. He deftly turned the fish with a spatula.

In seventeen minutes the rice was perfectly done, the fish were lying on paper towels on a platter, and the two men were perched on high stools, one on either side of the bar.

The bluegills were crispy brown on the outside but firm and steamy tender within. Bones are a problem with bluegills, but a welcome burden, Mulheisen felt, when the fish were cooked so well. The rice was delicious and the salad was crisp and tasty. Mulheisen wished the Chardonnay a bit cooler, but he deferred to his host's dental problems and, anyway, it was palatable.

Jon A. Jackson's most recent novel is *No Man's Dog*. Other recent novels include *Badger Games*, *La Donna Detroit*, *Hit on the House*, and *The Blind Pig*. He has been writing "Fang Mulheisen" crime novels since the publication of *The Diehard* in 1977.

WHEAT, RYE, and INDIAN BREAD

When the English arrived in North America in the 1600s they found corn but no oats, so they substituted one for the other. Rye soon entered the picture, because it grew better than wheat in the North. At first, wheat flour was too expensive for daily use, and it was reserved for special-occasion treats like cakes and pastries. But by the 1860s, settlers had discovered that it would grow well in the Midwest and that it could be transported cheaply by way of the Erie Canal, so they began using it for everyday baking.

Rye and Indian bread was a mainstay of the early colonists. I've taken the basic combination of cornmeal and rye flour, added wheat flour for gluten, and molasses for flavoring, a combination that was known as Third or Thirded Bread in the eighteenth and nineteenth centuries. This bread is dense, fine-crumbed, and flavorful.

The following is adapted from my cookbook, Baking in America, *published by Houghton Mifflin Publishing Company in 2002.*

○ ○

1 cup stone-ground **yellow cornmeal**

2 cups **water**

1 cup **milk** *(any fat content)*

$\frac{1}{2}$ cup **molasses**

2 cups **light rye flour**

2 to 3 cups **bread flour** or **unbleached all-purpose flour,** plus more as needed

2 cups **whole wheat flour**

1 package (2$\frac{1}{4}$ teaspoons) fast-rise **dry yeast**

1 tablespoon table **salt**
Makes 2 large loaves.

1. In a saucepan, combine the cornmeal with 1 cups water and milk. Cook over medium heat, stirring, until the mixture boils and thickens. Cook 2 more minutes. Remove from the heat and stir in the remaining 1 cup water and the molasses. Transfer to a mixing bowl. Stir occasionally until cornmeal is warm to the touch and transfer to bowl of stand mixer.

2. Add the rye flour, 2 cups bread flour, whole wheat flour, yeast, and salt. With dough hook, knead on medium-low speed for 5 minutes until wet and sticky. Add $\frac{1}{2}$ cup more bread flour and knead for 5 more minutes until the dough is firm but slightly sticky. Add remaining $\frac{1}{2}$ cup flour as necessary.

If making by hand, to warm cornmeal mixture, stir in rye flour, whole wheat flour, yeast, and salt. Add 2 cups bread flour and stir. Sprinkle another $\frac{1}{2}$ cup bread flour on work surface. Scrape dough onto it, dust with remaining $\frac{1}{2}$ cup bread flour. Knead 8 to 10 minutes until firm and slightly sticky.

Put dough in a lightly oiled, 6-quart bowl and turn to coat all surfaces. Cover with plastic wrap and let rise until the dough has doubled, about 2 hours.

3. Transfer the dough to a lightly floured surface, flatten slightly, and halve. Shape each half into a ball. Pinch seams on the underside of the balls to seal. Shape dough into rectangular loaves and place seam side down into two greased 9-inch by 5-inch loaf pans. Cover loosely with oiled plastic wrap, and let dough rise until double, about 2 hours.

4. About 30 minutes before bread is ready to bake, adjust an oven rack to the lower third position and preheat the oven to 375°.

5. To bake bread, remove plastic wrap and place pans in the oven. Bake 35 to 45 minutes, until loaves sound hollow when removed from pans and rapped on their bottoms. Cool bread out of pans on wire racks.

6. Cut the cooled bread with a sharp serrated knife. Bread keeps well for 3 or 4 days; store leftovers in a brown paper bag.

Greg Patent has published *New Frontiers in Western Cooking, A is for Apple* (co-written with his wife, Dorothy) and *Baking in America,* which won the 2003 James Beard Award. He has written regularly for *Cooking Light, Fine Cooking, Saveur,* and *Bon Appétit.* He writes a monthly food column for the *Missoulian* and cohosts a weekly food show with mystery writer Jon Jackson at noon Sundays on Montana Public Radio.

SWEET POTATO CORNBREAD

This is not your everyday average dry-as-hell cornbread.

1½ cups **yellow cornmeal**

1½ cups **white flour**

2 tablespoons **baking powder**

¼ teaspoon **cinnamon**

¼ teaspoon **cardamom**

1 teaspoon **salt**

1 cup **butter**

½ cup **brown sugar**

2 **eggs**

2 tablespoons **orange juice**

2 cups cooked, mashed **sweet potatoes**

½ cup **skim milk** or **non-dairy milk**

1 cup **frozen corn** (thawed)

Makes about 16 slices.

1. Preheat oven to 350º.

2. Combine dry ingredients in large mixing bowl.

3. In a mixer, cream butter until fluffy (about 1 minute). Add brown sugar and mix briefly. Add eggs, orange juice, sweet potatoes, and milk. Mix until smooth.

4. Add dry ingredients and mix well. Fold in corn. Coat two 9-inch pans with cooking spray and pour batter into them. Bake about 20 to 30 minutes until firm or until cake tester inserted in center comes out clean. Cool before serving.

Michael Earl Craig's first book of poems is *Can You Relax in My House.* He lives in the Shields Valley, north of Livingston, with his wife, dog, and mule, and works as a professional farrier.

WHOLE GRAIN BREAD or WRITER'S MANNA

My mom bakes a variety of fresh breads for our family. This is my favorite. One bite of a warm toasted slice, dripping with butter and honey, makes me smile—even when I'm tangled in a knotted sentence.

○○

1. Place $\frac{1}{2}$ cup warm water in a large mixing bowl. Add yeast and let sit a few minutes until it dissolves and bubbles.

2. Mix remaining $1\frac{1}{2}$ cups warm water, honey, and plain yogurt. Add to yeast mixture.

3. Vigorously stir in sunflower seeds, flax seeds, and 2 cups whole wheat flour. Let mixture sit 30 minutes or until bubbly. Stir in salt and all additional flour (1 cup whole wheat and 3 cups white). Add flour or water as needed to make a firm dough. Knead 10 minutes or until smooth and elastic.

4. Press dough into a patty. Break the butter into bits and push into the dough. Knead again until butter is completely incorporated.

5. Place dough in an oiled bowl. Cover and let rise until double, about 2 hours.

6. Preheat oven to 350°. Divide dough in two. Press each piece into a rectangle. Roll up and place in 2 greased bread pans. Let rise until tops rise gently over tops of the pans. Bake for 35 to 40 minutes or until golden brown on top.

2 cups **warm water**

1 shy tablespoon **dry yeast**
(*or one package*)

$\frac{1}{4}$ cup **honey**

$\frac{1}{2}$ cup **plain yogurt**

$\frac{1}{4}$ cup **sunflower seeds,** chopped or whole

$\frac{1}{4}$ cup **flax seeds,** chopped or whole

3 cups **whole wheat flour**

$2\frac{3}{4}$ teaspoons **salt**

3 cups unbleached **white flour**

2 to 3 tablespoons **butter**

Makes 2 loaves.

Christopher Paolini

Christopher Paolini was born on November 17, 1983, in southern California. Aside from a couple of years in Anchorage, Alaska, he has spent his entire life in Paradise Valley, Montana, where he still resides. He lives with his parents and younger sister, Angela, in a rustic two-story farmhouse on the banks of the Yellowstone River. They have two pets, Otis, a black-and-white cat, and Annie, a frisky cocker/Australian shepherd mix.

The tall, jagged Beartooth Mountains rise on one side of the Paradise Valley. Snowcapped most of the year, they inspired the fantastic scenery in Christopher Paolini's book, *Eragon*. A few years ago, Christopher hiked to the top of one peak and could see the Grand Teton mountain range, 100 miles to the south.

Christopher was home-schooled by his parents. He often wrote short stories and poems in an attempt to put his thoughts into words. He made frequent trips to the library and read widely. Some of his favorite books were Bruce Colville's *Jeremy Thatcher, Dragon Hatcher*, Frank Herbert's *Dune*, Raymond E. Feist's *Magician*, and Philip Pullman's *His Dark Materials*, as well as books by Anne McCaffrey, Jane Yolen, Brian Jacques, E. R. Eddison, David Eddings, and Ursula Le Guin.

Christopher grew up listening to a variety of music, but classical music fired his imagination and helped him write. He often listened to Mahler, Beethoven, and Wagner while writing *Eragon*. The final battle of *Eragon* was written while listening to *Carmina Burana*, by Carl Orff.

The story of *Eragon* began as the daydreams of a teen. Christopher wanted to try his hand at telling a story that included all the things he enjoyed in other fantasy novels. The project began as a hobby; he never intended it to be published. He took a month to plot out the entire trilogy, then sat on the sofa and began writing in a notebook. When he reached sixty pages, he gained enough confidence to transfer his work to his Macintosh computer, where most of

Eragon was written, although he sometimes found that the story flowed better when he wrote by hand. All the characters in *Eragon* are from Christopher's imagination except Angela the herbalist, who is loosely based on his sister.

It took him a year to write the first draft of *Eragon*. When Christopher first read the manuscript, he was appalled to discover how poorly it was written. The story was there, however, so he took a second year to revise the book and then gave it to his parents to read. They were astonished by the quality and unique voice of his work, and decided to help him release the book through the family's publishing company. A third year was spent with another round of edits, designing a cover, typesetting the manuscript, and creating marketing materials. During this time Christopher drew the map for *Eragon*, as well as the dragon eye that appears inside the hardcover edition. Finally, the manuscript was sent to press, and the first books arrived.

The Paolini family spent the next year promoting the book themselves. Beginning with presentations at the local library and high school, they then traveled across the United States. In all, Christopher gave over 135 presentations in libraries, bookstores, and schools in 2002 and early 2003. He did most of the presentations dressed in a medieval costume of red shirt, billowy black pants, lace-up boots, and a jaunty black cap.

In summer 2002, Carl Hiaasen, the author of *Hoot*, brought *Eragon* to the attention of his publisher, Alfred A. Knopf, who subsequently acquired the rights to publish *Eragon* and the rest of the Inheritance trilogy.

Christopher's next book, *Eldest* (Inheritance, Book II), will be published in fall 2005. He is promoting Eragon and consulting on the *Eragon* movie for Fox 2000. Once the trilogy is finished, Christopher plans to take a long vacation, when he will ponder which of his many story ideas he will write next.

Nora Martin

2 teaspoons **yeast**

1 tablespoon **honey** *(or more if you like your bread sweeter, up to 1/3 cup)*

1½ cups warm *(80-degree)* **water**

2 tablespoons **oil**

3 cups **whole wheat flour** plus extra for kneading

½ cup **gluten flour**

⅓ cup **oats**

5 tablespoons unsweetened **coconut**

5 tablespoons **sunflower seeds**

5 tablespoons **nuts**

1 teaspoon **salt**

MAMA'S HOMEMADE CAMP BREAD

From *Living at the Pine Creek Campground*

1. In a large ceramic bowl dissolve yeast and honey in warm water. Let stand for 5 minutes.

2. Add oil and stir in whole wheat flour, gluten flour, oats, coconut, sunflower seeds, and nuts.

3. Flour a board and turn out dough. Knead in more flour as needed to form a dough that is not sticky. Knead 100 times or until dough is soft and elastic.

4. Cover bowl with clean cloth and let rise for 45 minutes in a warm place.

5. Punch down dough.

6. Divide dough in two. Form loaves and place in greased bread pans or french bread tubes. Cover and let rise 30 minutes.

7. Preheat oven to 350°.

8. Bake for 25 minutes.

From Nora Martin's novel *Living at the Pine Creek Campground.*

Pine Creek is a bitsy sneeze of a place in the mountains of eastern Oregon. They're called the Wallowa Mountains. If you were looking down from the sky they would look like the bumpy backs of a bunch of giant sleeping porcupines that are all lying in a chaotic heap, nose to tail, north to south, east to west, every which-way through the dry eastern side of the state. The porcupines' quills are the forests of lodge pole and white pine trees. So you can see that Pine Creek is a fitting name for where we ended up.

The Pine Creek Campground itself is like a little town made of miniature buildings, some squatting on wheels, some just perched on the bare ground. They are scattered among the big rocks and trees that line the edge of the creek itself. There are lots of little cubbyholes to pitch tents and park camp trailers in. There is a cabin that is both reception office and communal kitchen. There is also a big covered porch with a nice old rock fireplace in it and splintery wood benches that will seat everyone in the camp at once, even in summer when we are full to the brim with happy vacationers.

There are not many of us that live here year round, but together we make everything we need. Mama sells a few groceries in the Camp office, things such as: coffee, colas (cold in the winter, warm in the summer), and soap. She also sells her special homemade camp bread and blackberry jam that she cooks and jars in the communal camp-ground kitchen.

People are always welcome to come and sit around in the rickety chairs next to the wood stove in the Pine Creek Campground office. You could say it's almost like a town café. The coffeepot is always on. Mama and Granny Kretchley keep a plate of goodies on the counter where anyone can help themselves. And they are even known to make a whole herd of sandwiches for people who need some lunch in them. There is a chessboard on a stump, and the whole building smells like piney wood smoke and homemade bread.

Nora Martin writes: I spent my childhood years exploring the coast of Washington State. The islands, woods, mountains, birds, and animals fascinated me. On one of my missions, I found a dead kingfisher bird and thought it was the most beautiful treasure. Of course, I took it in to my second grade class for show and tell. The teacher, as well as the students, did not share my opinion, especially when the smell of dead bird filled the classroom. But in spite of that, nature has always been magical for me.

Besides writing, I have the pleasure of sharing my life with my husband, Andy, and two sons, Winslow and Haynes, and of course, Tex the cat and Hughie the Lovebird. I am the librarian in a rural Montana elementary school. I also teach classes in literature and library science at Montana State University.

The best thing about a writing life is that it serves as a vehicle from which you can view your life. I hope that recording time passing by allows me to savor this spectacular life. From the silhouettes of trees at night, to owls and insects, I long to know it all.

BRAN MUFFINS

Marian Abbot, newspaper photographer and Women's Editor for the Daily Interlake; gardener extraordinaire; grower of apples; spry, white-haired widow and smoker of cigarettes, lived in a little white house across the street from my family in Kalispell, Montana. We called her Miss Apple. She fed us. She made us famous. The recipe is hers, one of my favorites. The photograph is hers, too, Melanie Rae, age four, dressed as a monarch butterfly for Kalispell's Halloween parade. My mother made the outfit. My mother transformed me. When I am in despair, I conjure this image and remember: Anything is possible. I like the skeleton, too, the way it reveals what's inside, what we all become, what is secret and beautiful. Miss Apple's photo appeared on the front page of the Daily Interlake, October 31, 1961. Marian Abbot died August 29, 2004, age 101. God bless her.

Recipe from the kitchen of Marian Abbot

○ ○

1. Preheat oven to 400°.

2. Stir together dry ingredients.

3. Mix egg, milk, molasses, and olive oil and add to dry mixture. Fold in raisins. Bake in greased muffin cups 20 to 30 minutes. Test with toothpick.

1 cup **whole wheat pastry flour**

1 teaspoon **baking soda**

1½ cups **raw wheat bran**

1 **egg**

¾ cup **milk**

½ cup **molasses**

2 tablespoons **extra light virgin olive oil**

½ cup **raisins** *(rinsed)*

Makes 12 muffins.
Hallelujah! Six for the Thons, and six for Miss Apple.

I chose this short excerpt because it evokes the idea that food restores us, even saves us, echoing the way the butterfly photograph juxtaposes the happy child with the skeleton. I hope the scene illuminates the spiritual importance of food, especially when another person offers it to us as a gift—as dear Miss Apple did so many times.

From "*Letters in the Snow*," published in *One Story*, May 30, 2005.

Dear Kirk and Trudie Iyler,

I lived in your elegant cabin above Swan Lake for twenty-eight hours. You were courteous and wise to leave a spare key where I could find it. I busted no locks; I broke no windows. I swear I had a vision: a tall man tipping a clay flowerpot on the porch, a slender red-haired woman sliding a key on a yellow string under it.

I tipped the pot, and there it was, the key and all it promised.

You are clean people, you and your three grown children: Lance, Duncan, Amanda. I saw their names and numbers on the refrigerator and wanted to call them. I thought I'd say, *I'm your cousin, Nicole. I'm at the cabin. Come get me.*

I found the breaker box in the bedroom closet and parted your clothes to flip the switches for your pump and hot water. It took hours for the water to heat. I heard the hum and groan, the song of pipes expanding. *Trudie!* It was worth the wait, every minute. If it's true God is everywhere in everything, he was the warm water in your bathtub. God the womb. God the mother.

I meant to be considerate, to hang your towels and wash your dishes. I meant to turn your heaters off, and now, I know, your warmth is wasted. Forgive me. The tracks through your house are my confession: *The bad sister of Goldilocks was here. I rumpled your bed. I devoured your porridge.* I ate a whole can of pork & beans. I slurped three bowls of instant oatmeal. If I survive another night, know that your food has become my flesh. Know that you have saved me.

Melanie Rae Thon's most recent book is the novel *Sweet Hearts*, published by Washington Square Press in 2002. She is also the author of *Meteors in August and Iona Moon*, and the story collections *First, Body* and *Girls in the Grass*. Originally from Montana, she now divides her time between the Pacific Northwest and Salt Lake City, where she teaches at the University of Utah.

HOTCAKES

When my grandfather was first living alone in Missoula in the early 1930s, his mother, Carrie Meloy, sent him recipes he could make for himself. This is her pancake recipe as she wrote it out for him. I use buttermilk and the optional egg.

1 cup **flour**

1 teaspoon **salt**

1 tablespoon **sugar**

 Sour milk or **buttermilk**

1 teaspoon **baking soda**

$\frac{1}{4}$ cup hot **water**

1 **egg**

 Enough for 2 unless very big eaters.

1. Combine flour, sugar and salt.

2. Mix smooth and rather stiff with sour milk or buttermilk.

3. Put one teaspoon of baking soda a little better than level full in a cup and pour some hot water on it—maybe a quarter of a cup of hot water. Stir until dissolved. Pour this in batter and stir well by beating, thin down with sour milk until it will pour from spoon or pitcher or whatever you mix it in.

4. The addition of an egg well beaten helps them but they are good enough without the egg.

5. If you want to increase this recipe, just use more flour and more salt, sugar, and soda.

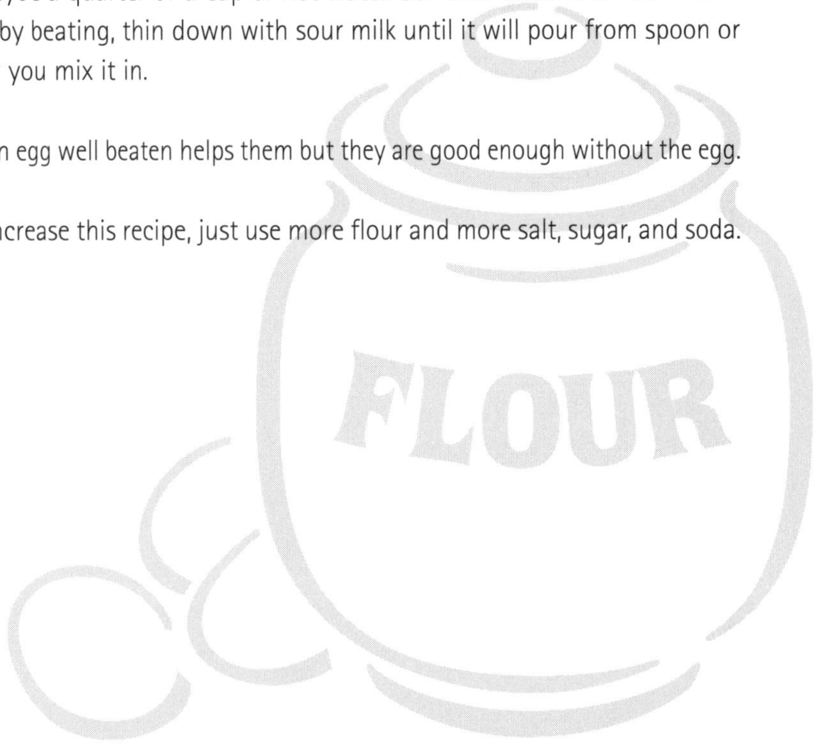

From "Travis, B.," first published in the *New Yorker* in October 2002.

In the café, the waitress slid a burger and fries in front of Beth Travis and said, "The cook wants to know if that's your horse out back."

Chet said it was.

"Can he give it some water?"

He said he'd appreciate it.

"Truck break down?" the waitress asked.

He said no, his truck was all right, and the waitress went away.

Beth Travis turned the long end of the oval plate in his direction, and took up the burger. "Have some fries," she said. "How come you never eat anything?"

He wanted to say that he wasn't hungry when he was around her, but he feared the look on her face if he said it, the way she would shy away.

"Why were you afraid of selling shoes?" he asked.

"Have you ever sold shoes? It's hell."

"I mean why were you afraid you couldn't get anything else?"

She looked at the burger as if the answer was in there. Her eyes were almost the same color as her hair, and ringed with pale lashes. He wondered if she thought of him as an Indian boy, with his mother's dark hair. "I don't know," she said. "Yes, I do know. Because my mother works in a school cafeteria, and my sister works in a hospital laundry, and selling shoes is the nicest job a girl from my family is supposed to get."

"What about your father?"

"I don't know him."

"That's a sad story."

"No, it's not," she said.

Maile Meloy was born and raised in Helena, Montana. She is the author of the story collection *Half in Love* and the novel *Liars and Saints*. Her stories have been published in the *New Yorker* and *The Paris Review*, and she received a Guggenheim Fellowship in 2004. She lives in California.

DUPA

Dupa, *a Swedish egg gravy, is a family recipe from the old country, so old country that ingredients and attitudes give the best epicurial effect. My 12-year-old daughter suggested the recipe for* dupa *remain in the Gustafson family, so much does she treasure the breakfast delight. She made me ask my father if it was okay to share the Rapelje's Montana dish with the world. Grandpa Rib thought it might be all right as long as I didn't mention his secret ingredient, which is any secret ingredient you might want to add.*

Dupa *is a variable sort of delight. A maker of gravies is best suited as the chef, as many consistencies and degrees of smoothness can result, depending on the gravy-maker. Patience is a virtue in making such a dish.* Dupa *is spread over buttered toast and eaten with a knife and fork, European style.*

Side pork from a free-range pig, cooked to a certain gourmet crispiness, can be served as a side dish. The use of the crumbles from the drippings can flavor the gravy (my secret ingredient that is added during the heating of the olive oil). Lutefisk was once considered an appropriate side dish when Swedes once lived next to the ocean, but it fell out of favor until it was found that, in eastern Montana, lutefisk could be used to keep skunks from raising their young under one's house. Lutefisk was simply placed around the foundation and skunks stayed clear. The only problem was that the Swedes employing the tactic were overrun by Norwegians, and that was no fun at all. "You can always tell a Norwegian," my Grandma Gus always told me as she stirred her dupa, *"but you yust can't tell them much."*

○ ○

4 **eggs** from happy chickens—the bright-yellow-yolked variety give the most pleasing color to this milk-and-egg sauce

$\frac{1}{4}$ cup **olive oil**

About $\frac{1}{4}$ cup **flour**—Wondra is good

About $1\frac{1}{2}$ cups of **milk** from one happy backyard cow

Serves 2 to 3.

This is a low-temperature cooking experience, the heat incrementally reduced as the gravy thickens.

1. Crack eggs in a bowl and whip them up with a fork, getting a good share of air into them.

2. In a cast iron or stainless steel pan, heat the olive oil. A thick sheen across the pan is usually enough, but don't be stingy with it.

3. Add some flour and stir with a whisk. Continue to whisk until the flour gets a bit cooked, and keep stirring. Don't be leaving the *dupa* to butter the toast.

4. After the flour and oil sets up to your satisfaction, add the milk and keep stirring.

5. When the mixture starts steaming, stir in the eggs and continue whisking 3, 4, or 5 minutes—there are many degrees of smoothness.

6. When the gravy is smooth and the eggs cooked to your satisfaction remove the pan from the low heat and continue stirring. Pour the sauce into a bowl and serve over buttered toast. Condiments include sea salt, of course, and pepper—black and cayenne.

Dupa *means dip in Swedish, and the old-country farm folk from Smöland simply tore their bread apart and dipped it into the gravy. Since the advent of sliced bread, my homestead ancestors have taken to buttering toast, spreading the gravy over, and eating the dish with a fork, à la biscuits-and-gravy. One branch of Gustafsons uses untoasted bread. Any bread can be used—white bread, bagels, biscuits, or croissants. Whole wheat varieties are encouraged. Organic is good.*

Coffee and orange juice are good beverages to accompany dupa, and a good walk afterwards keeps the cholesterol from sticking. Curdling may result if the heat is turned too high or you leave the gravy unattended to butter the toast. For those of you with chickens in the backyard, this dish is a must.

Sid Gustafson is the author of the novel *Prisoners of Flight*, published by Permanent Press in 2003. He lives in Bozeman, where he practices veterinary medicine. His novel *Horsemen* will be published in 2006.

Lois Welch

1 loaf day-old **French bread,** cut in 1-inch cubes

8 ounces **Jarlsberg** or **Gruyère cheese**, grated

1 cup **whipping cream**

1 cup **white wine**

$\frac{1}{4}$ teaspoon **cayenne pepper** (optional)

Serves 3.

NEWSPAPER FAKE FONDUE

1. Preheat oven to 375°.

2. Fill a buttered casserole with the cubed French bread.

3. Combine rest of ingredients in bowl and mix well.

4. Pour half of the mixture over bread. Allow bread to soak up mixture, then pour in the rest, allowing plenty of grated cheese to remain on top.

5. Bake 25 minutes, until fondue is puffed up and brown. Serve immediately with a fruit salad and white wine.

Recipe notes: No day-old French bread? Get a fresh loaf of sourdough or regular French bread. Heat oven to 250°. Slice loaf, tear into pieces, and spread on cookie sheet. Dry in oven for 7 to 10 minutes. I cut the cheese into 1-inch by $\frac{1}{2}$-inch cubes and whirl it in my food processor. Sometimes I rub the casserole with a cut clove of garlic before buttering it. The cheese, cream, and wine mixture can be made ahead.

Finish the fruit salad while the fondue bakes or make the fruit salad ahead and serve a cold artichoke as a first course while the fondue bakes.

Double the recipe if you are serving more than 3 people. You can multiply indefinitely; the trick to flavor is keeping the half-cream/half-wine mixture proportion.

From *The Heartsong of Charging Elk*, published by Doubleday Publishing Company in 2000.

After a tour of the rest of the flat, they had tea in the parlor. Madame Soulas served honey-soaked cakes on small china plates. She was not quite sure what the *Indien* would do with his, but he ate it with a fork. She didn't know that Broncho Billy and the reservation Indians had taught him how to eat his food from a plate with a knife and fork. They had laughed at him when he speared his piece of roasted meat with his own knife and bit a large hunk from it.

Finally, it was Sees Twice who told him to put the meat back on the plate, then showed him how to cut it with the many-pronged fork and the dull knife which lay beside the plate. That was in the train station in Omaha and it was the first of many times that Charging Elk had wished that he had never left the Stronghold.

Franklin Bell watched Charging Elk eat the sweetcake and he was surprised at how deliberately, how delicately the Indian ate. He made the sweetcake last a long time. And he didn't touch his tea until the cake was gone. Then he sipped it down, carefully replacing the cup and saucer on the table.

Bell wondered if all the Indians in the Wild West show had such good table manners.

Lois Welch grew up in Salem, Oregon. After getting her BA at Willamette University, where she acquired a taste for French culture and cuisine as an *assistante de langue anglaise* in French, she earned her MA and PhD in comparative literature at Occidental College in Los Angeles. She taught four years at Portland State University before joining the English department at the University of Montana in 1966. In 1968 she married James Welch; they cooked and sampled French cuisine together for the next 35 years. She directed the creative writing program for 8 years, and headed the English department for 3 years. She retired in 2001 and currently lives in Missoula.

Born in Browning in 1940, James Welch was an enrolled member of the Blackfeet Tribe. He attended schools on the Blackfeet and Fort Belknap reservations, received his BA from the University of Montana in 1965, and spent two years in the MFA program in creative writing studying with acclaimed poet Richard Hugo. He published one book of poems, *Riding the Earthboy 40*, which was recently re-issued Carnegie-Mellon University Press. The recipient of numerous literary awards and honorary doctorates, Welch published five novels, *Winter in the Blood*, *The Death of Jim Loney*, *Fools Crow*, *The Indian Lawyer*, and *The Heartsong of Charging Elk*, as well as a book of nonfiction, *Killing Custer*. He died in 2003.

LENNON'S BEANS and RICE

I've eaten this meal once a week since 1993, when a fellow MFA student, Mark Holthoff, taught me a version of it. I have written 6 books under its influence and anything good about them is probably attributable to it.

○ ○

1 tablespoon **olive oil**

2 slices **bacon,** chopped

1 small **onion,** chopped

1 large clove **garlic,** minced

1 teaspoon **chili powder**

1 can favorite **beans** *(or 1 cup soaked and cooked beans)*

1 medium **tomato,** chopped

Tamari sauce

1 cup grated **Monterey Jack cheese**

2 cups cooked **brown rice**

Serves 3.

1. Get brown rice cooking first—it takes an hour.

2. With 35 minutes to go until dinnertime, pour olive oil into a medium saucepan. Add bacon, onion, garlic, and chili powder. Cook attentively over medium-high heat, stirring often, until bacon is crisp, onions and garlic are soft, and chili powder has given everything a grainy deep-red hue. Remove from heat.

3. Drain the beans, then add them and the chopped tomato to onion mixture. Add tamari sauce to taste (careful!). Mix thoroughly, then take your masher or a heavy fork and mash everything in one side of the pan to a coarse paste. Mix it all up again, cover, and return to heat.

4. The moment the mixture begins to simmer, reduce heat to low and half-cover. Simmer for 30 minutes, stirring every 5 minutes or so to make sure it isn't sticking to the bottom of the pan. When the half hour is up, spread over a bed of rice and sprinkle the cheese on top. Wordlessly devour.

"Last Meal," an anecdote from the book *Pieces for the Left Hand*: *100 Anecdotes*, published by Granta Press in 2005.

Our many trips to a local diner have resulted in our acquaintance with a short order cook, a man in his late thirties whose intensive self-training and obsessive attention to detail have resulted in an uncanny ability to make, from such rudiments as eggs, potatoes, meatloaf and cold cuts, rough-hewn delicacies of surprising originality and variety. So pleased does he seem while at work, and so satisfied with his creations, that we were once given to ask if he'd ever made a meal he didn't like.

After some thought, he told us that he had once been employed as the head chef at a state prison, where one night he was asked to cook a last meal for a murderer who had been condemned to death. The murderer had requested a porterhouse steak, medium rare; french fries; a bowl of raspberry sherbet and a glass of iced tea. As per state prison regulations, it was also required that he be served a green salad. The prisoner was to be executed at midnight and would be served dinner at 7:30pm, after the other inmates were through eating.

Though he had little sympathy for the murderer, the cook was opposed to capital punishment and decided to make the meal a special one. He chose an excellent cut of meat and prepared it with a thick, hearty mushroom gravy; he seasoned the fries lightly with paprika and garlic powder and made the sherbet by hand, with real fruit, in an ice-cream maker he brought from home. The iced tea he brewed several hours in the sun, using the finest first-flush Darjeeling he could find, and he garnished it with lemon and a sprig of mint. The salad contained no fewer than six fresh, flavorful greens.

Unfortunately, the meal was returned to the kitchen barely touched, the meat gone cold and tough, the sherbet melted and the fries congealed and pasty. The cook was devastated. It was bad enough, he told us, that he had made an unpalatable meal, but far worse that he had, in the process, ruined a condemned man's final hours. My wife and I immediately pointed out that the meal might well have been wonderful, but the man's life was about to end, and he was likely too lost in thoughts of death to eat. The cook said that this was nice of us to suggest, but he knew the truth, and would regret that meal for the rest of his life.

Since then we have always, after eating at the diner, commented generously on the high quality of our food.

J. Robert Lennon has written four novels and a collection of very short stories. He learned to do this in Missoula, Montana, and now lives in Ithaca, New York.

Stephenie Ambrose Tubbs

1 pound **pork sausage**

5 **celery stalks** with tops, diced

1 **onion,** diced

2 cloves **garlic,** minced

1 can **red beans**

Tabasco, salt, and **pepper** to taste

Prepared rice for 4

Serves 4

Stephenie Ambrose Tubbs is a coauthor of *The Lewis and Clark Companion: An Encyclopedic Guide to the Voyage of Discovery*. She is a Montana historian and serves on the Lewis and Clark National Trail Interpretive Center's Foundation Board, and is the daughter of the late Stephen Ambrose.

AMBROSE'S UNDAUNTED RED BEANS and RICE

A traditional New Orleans dish usually served on Mondays or wash day.

○○○

1. Brown sausage and drain most of the fat. Mix in celery and onion.

2. Cook till translucent. Add garlic and red beans.

3. Simmer for several hours adding water as needed.

4. Before serving, mash some of the beans to make a creamier sauce.

5. Serve over rice.

○○○

From *The Lewis and Clark Companion: An Encyclopedic Guide to the Voyage of Discovery* by Stephenie Ambrose Tubbs and Clay Jenkinson, published by Henry Holt and Company in 2003.

Dog: A frequent source of protein for the men of the expedition, which purchased 193 dogs for its own consumption. As Lewis commented at Fort Clatsop, "our party from necessaty having been obliged to subsist some length of time on dogs have now become extreemly fond of their flesh; it is worthy of remark that while we lived principally on the flesh of this anamal we were much more healthy strong and more fleshey than we had been since we left the Buffaloe country. For my own part I have become so reconciled to the dog that I think it agreeable food and would prefer it vastly to lean Venison or Elk" Captain Clark was the only man who did not appreciate the taste of dog, stating, "I have not become reconsiled to the taste of this animal yet."

COSNINO CHILI

1. Dredge meat in flour.

2. In a Dutch oven or large heavy saucepan, sauté meat in oil or lard until lightly browned. Transfer to plate.

3. Sauté onion, garlic, and chiles in same pan until onion is slightly wilted.

4. Return meat to pan and add remaining ingredients.

5. Add water to cover and simmer for 2 to 3 hours or until tender.

○ ○

From "Big Lost River Breakdown," unpublished.

"Whatever happens in this mangled world,"
Grandpa says, "the good cookin' goes on.
Everybody knows you got to feed both body and soul."
Grandpa came out from Kentucky, can't remember
the story, maybe with the military, maybe
his truck broke down in Arco. Weeks passed,
going nowhere. Then the smell of those ribs
cooking cast a spell over the neighborhood,
drifted up the highway past the city limit sign,
enough to make a hungry person sigh.

Greg Pape is the author of *Border Crossings*, *Storm Pattern*, and *Sunflower Facing the Sun*. His most recent book, *American Flamingo*, received the Crab Orchard Award, and his book *Black Branches* was reprinted in the Carnegie Mellon Classic Contemporaries series. He teaches in the writing program at the University of Montana and in the brief-residency MFA program at Spalding University.

2 pounds **venison** *(or pork or beef)*, cut into 1-inch cubes

Flour

¼ cup **olive oil, lard,** or other **shortening**

1 large **onion,** chopped

2 cloves **garlic,** peeled and minced

4 **Anaheim chiles,** roasted, peeled, and chopped *(or 2 or 3 4-ounce cans of green chiles, sliced)*

1 16-ounce can **white hominy**

3 or 4 diced **potatoes**

1 teaspoon **oregano**

1 teaspoon **cumin**

1 teaspoon dried **cilantro** or fresh cilantro

1 teaspoon **salt**

1 teaspoon **chili powder** *(optional or add more to taste)*

¼ cup **red wine** or ½ cup **beer**

Serves 6.

John Holbrook

2 tablespoons **olive oil**

1 large **onion,** diced

3 **garlic cloves,** minced

2 cans **chicken stock**

2 boneless **chicken breasts,** cooked and cut into chunks

6 cans small **white beans,** with liquid

8 fresh **tomatillos,** washed, peeled, and sliced

1 can **green chiles,** diced

1 large **red bell pepper,** washed and diced

$\frac{1}{2}$ teaspoon **cumin**

$\frac{1}{2}$ teaspoon **oregano**

Juice from 1 freshly squeezed **lime**

4 to 6 tablespoons **fresh cilantro,** finely chopped

Fresh ground **pepper** to taste

Cayenne *(if you want to kick up heat index)*

Serves 4.

CHILI BLANCO

1. Heat olive oil in pan; add onion, cook till clear, not browned, 3 to 5 minutes. Add garlic, cook additional 2 minutes.

2. Place onions, garlic, and oil in large crock pot or similar vessel.

3. Add chicken stock, chicken chunks, small white beans, tomatillos, green chilis, red bell pepper, cumin, oregano, lime juice, chopped cilantro, ground pepper, and cayenne (if desired). Additional salt is not necessary as salt in stock and beans plus lime flavor is sufficient.

4. Stir and cover. Cook until bubbling, then turn heat to low and cook 3 to 4 hours. Serve with buttered hard rolls, and a small salad. Freezes and reheats nicely. Enjoy.

From *Clear Water on the Swan*, First Book Award, Montana Arts Council, 1991.

Whiteout
A cold hard wind,
a howling of snow,
a chinook blows out,
thermometers drop,
wind chills soar.

Whiteout. Sky,
hills, barrow pit,
home, —all the same.
I know which way to go:
I gun it and coast,

give it a boost then glide,
balancing the wheel
with the tips of my fingers,
right on along down
the tightrope-like crown of the road.

*Why have I chosen this poem? Well, thinking
about a steaming crock of Chili Blanco waiting
for me at the end of the road—keeping me going—
is about as good a reason as any.*

John Holbrook lives and writes in Missoula, Montana. He and his wife, Judith, a couple of just-beyond-middle-age but still-proud-once-upon-a-time hippies (near hobbits, who never had many wild adventures!), recently celebrated 37 years of marriage. John's poetry chapbook, *Loose Wool, River Tackle, Pencil Drafts*, was published by House Publications in 2002. He shared the Montana Arts Council's 1991 First Book Award for *Clear Water On the Swan*, and his poems have appeared in *Anataeus, The Carolina Quarterly, The Nebraska Review, Poetry Northwest*, and numerous other journals.

67

PENNE ALL' ARRABBIATA

I've included this recipe and excerpt because they represent a particular aspect of my family's mythology: the move from a rural/agrarian lifestyle defined by poverty and lack of opportunity to a new awareness of the world, including the pleasure one can take in food beyond its simple ability to provide sustenance.

4 tablespoons **olive oil**

2 to 3 **garlic cloves,** finely chopped

2 ounces **pancetta**

1½ cups **plum tomatoes,** chopped

2 to 3 **parsley sprigs**

Pinch of hot **red pepper flakes** or crumbled **dried red pepper**

Salt

1 pound **penne**

2 to 3 ounces grated **pecorino**

Freshly grated **parmigiano**

Serves 4.

The sauce:

1. Heat oil in a saucepan or skillet.

2. Add garlic and sauté over low heat for 1 minute until it begins to soften but not brown.

3. Increase the heat slightly and add pancetta. Brown on both sides.

4. Add tomatoes, parsley, hot pepper, and salt to taste.

5. Cover and cook over moderate heat for 20 minutes. Discard the pancetta and parsley.

To serve:

1. Cook penne in boiling water until al dente.

2. Drain and add to sauce.

3. Add Pecorino and cook for 2 minutes over high heat, stirring to coat.
Serve with grated Parmigiano, a loaf of crusty bread, and a good bottle of rioja.

From *Finding Caruso*, published by Putnam in 2003.

In this section, Buddy, a man looking back on the summer he turned seventeen, is sharing a meal with an older woman named Irene at Paulie's, an Italian restaurant located in Idaho. (The restaurant was inspired by a real restaurant, the Italian Gardens, which once thrived in Lewiston, Idaho, where my father, a young man who had come to Idaho to work as a logger, always chose fried chicken over the unfamiliar plate of pasta.)

Irene stepped out into the parking lot, led me through the entryway with its trellised partition woven with plastic grapevines. I could smell her—buttered toast, summer wheat, peach jam spiked with cinnamon. I knew that if I were to reach out, slide my hand beneath her hair, it would be heavy and hot with sun.

Paulie stood behind the cash register, counting his lunchtime take. He had the look of an immigrant Swede, big-jowled and flushed. His last name was Gertonson, but he claimed to have learned to make lasagna from his Italian grandmother. He seemed to recognize Irene and smiled broadly, then directed us to a corner table spread with a red-and-white cloth, handed us each a menu bound in cracked vinyl.

"Our special today," he announced, rubbing his hands down the white apron tied high on the mound of his middle, "is penne all' arrabbiata, but it is not for the timid." He spoke like a man uncomfortable with English. He looked at Irene and then at me. "We also have fried chicken."

"Oh, heavens, no." Irene looked at Paulie. "I think we should go with the chef's recommendation. Don't you, Buddy?"

Paulie brightened.

I'd been keen on the fried chicken, which I hadn't had since leaving Oklahoma. There'd been great platters of it at the funeral, bowls of potato salad, baked beans and slaw. I'd thought my grief would disallow any pleasure, but I'd eaten with an appetite that seemed insatiable, clearing plate after plate....

"What's the penny stuff got in it?" I asked.

"You'll like it, Buddy. And we need a bottle of wine. A good one."

Kim Barnes received an MFA from the University of Montana in 1995. She is the author of the memoir *In the Wilderness: Coming of Age in Unknown Country*, which was honored with a Pacific Northwest Booksellers Award and was a finalist for the Pulitzer Prize and the PEN/Martha Albrand Award. *Hungry for the World*, her second memoir, was published by Villard in 2000. Her first novel, *Finding Caruso*, was published by Marian Wood Books/Putnam in 2003. She was coeditor, with Mary Clearman Blew, of *Circle of Women: An Anthology of Contemporary Western Women Writers* and, with Claire Davis, *True Stories from the Midlife Underground: Women Over 40 Write About Love, Life, Sex, and Aging*, forthcoming from Doubleday in 2006. Barnes teaches creative writing at the University of Idaho. She is currently serving as Idaho Writer-in-Residence.

Russell Chatham

The pasta:

4 cups all purpose **flour**

4 extra large **eggs**

Olive oil

The sauce:

2 quarts heavy **whipping cream**

2 ounces of **Marsala** *(additional to taste)*

Sea salt *(go easy and correct at the end)*

About two dozen whole **black peppercorns**

White pepper, several shakes

Red pepper *(cayenne),* several shakes.

1 teaspoon **garlic powder**

3 or 4 **bay leaves**

A good whack of **marjoram** and **thyme**. *Dried herbs work, but use a fresh bouquet garni if possible*

Handful of **Italian parsley,** very roughly chopped

3 **yellow onions,** roughly chopped

3 **carrots,** sliced

1 pat **butter**

The filling:

8 spicy **Italian sausages**

6 ounces roughly chopped **spinach** *(one 6-ounce bag)*

1 cup freshly grated **Parmigiano-Reggiano**

1 pound fresh, whole milk **ricotta**

ground **coriander seed**

nutmeg

sea salt and freshly ground **pepper**

Serves 2 cannelloni each for 6 people.

ITALIAN SAUSAGE and RICOTTA CANNELLONI

This is one of the most sensuous comfort dishes there is, but you cannot use the store-bought dried pasta tubes, as the difference between those and fresh pasta is like the difference between a hippopotamus and a mongoose. Besides, making fresh pasta dough is a lovely experience, which adds immensely to the satisfaction of creating the dish.

The pasta:

1. Put flour on a large wooden cutting board. Make a well in the middle, and add eggs and a drizzle of olive oil.

2. Mix with a fork, then gradually begin to pull in flour from the sides. After several minutes, a mass will form. At this point, take the mass and work it in your hands.

3. Now you must knead the dough for 6 minutes and that has always worked for me. Wrap the kneaded dough ball in plastic wrap, and let it sit for at least a half hour before using it.

4. The finished product you are looking for is thin sheets about 6-inches wide and maybe 7- or 8-inches long. To make these, you need a pasta machine, and the simple hand crank version is adequate. Unwrap the dough, and slice off a piece a half-inch thick. Pass it through the machine at the thickest setting (2). Double it over and pass it through again. You may want to do this several times.

5. Now narrow the opening to 4, and repeat.

6. Narrow it again to 6, and repeat. You may now want to cut your sheet in half, as you will be amazed at how large the dough becomes, especially after you pass it through the thinnest setting, which is 9.

7. Cook the sheets soon after they're made by boiling them in a large pot of salted water, which only takes 2 minutes at most. Rinse in cold water, pat dry, and they are now ready to use.

The sauce:

Most recipes for cannelloni call for a traditional béchamel, but by basing this one on heavy cream instead, you get more richness and flavor, and a nicer consistency.

1. Combine all ingredients except butter and simmer for 1 hour, uncovered, stirring frequently. This will melt the vegetables and otherwise incorporate all the flavors. It will also reduce the cream somewhat, so its consistency becomes that which nicely coats a spoon, just like the cookbooks are always telling us.

2. Turn off the heat and whisk in a big-ass pat of sweet butter and another ounce, no two, of Marsala. Correct the seasoning, especially the salt.

3. Let stand for half an hour, strain through a normal strainer, and serve. This sauce will keep in the refrigerator for many days.

The filling:

1. Poach 8 spicy Italian sausages until just done. Do not overcook. Cool and peel off casings. Grind them up using the fine blade on a meat grinder or meat-grinding attachment that fits onto a mixer.

2. To the ground meat, add 6 ounces of roughly chopped fresh spinach.

3. Add the freshly grated Parmigiano-Reggiano and then ricotta.

4. Mix ingredients together, and season with several shakes of ground coriander seed, nutmeg, sea salt, and freshly ground pepper. If the mixture seems too stiff, drizzle in some heavy cream until it is nice and smooth but has good body.

5. Spoon the mixture onto the sheets of pasta and roll into tubes $1\frac{1}{2}$-inches in diameter and 6 inches wide. The pasta can lap over itself.

6. Heat covered in the sauce until warm. Remember, you're not cooking anything here, only warming it up, so be careful.

7. Place the tubes on a plate and spoon sauce over them. Garnish with chopped Italian parsley and red pepper flakes. The ordinary kind will work, but if you can find Marash red pepper from Turkey, it's much classier and more flavorful.

Russell Chatham is a renowned landscape painter, restaurateur, author, and publisher, living in Livingston, Montana. His books include *Silent Seasons, The Angler's Coast, Dark Waters, Striped Bass on the Fly, One Hundred Paintings, The Missouri Headwaters,* and *Selected Lithographs.*

1 pound **ground round** *(venison, beef, bison, or ground turkey will work)*

1½ cups **onion,** chopped

4 cloves **garlic,** minced

1 to 2 tablespoons **olive oil**

4 fresh **tomatoes,** peeled and diced *(or 1 large can crushed tomatoes)*

2 small cans **tomato paste**

½ cup **water**

⅛ teaspoon **cayenne pepper**

1 to 2 tablespoons **oregano**

1 to 2 teaspoons **dried basil**

½ teaspoon **sage**

2 **bay leaves**

½ pound **mushrooms,** chopped *(optional)*

¼ teaspoon pepper

DANNY ON'S SPAGHETTI SAUCE

1. Brown the ground round.

2. Sauté onions and garlic in oil until golden, then add to the meat, along with the other ingredients. Mix well.

3. Bring to boil, then cover and reduce heat to low. Simmer up to 3 hours.

4. Serve over spaghetti noodles with Parmesan cheese, a green salad, and good bread.

○○

From *All This Rain*, a novel in progress.

Nyna had never had sweet potatoes before, and she decided she liked them, especially the way Aunt Lois had fixed them with baby marshmallows on top. But that was about the only thing she liked, besides the turkey. There was a mixture of watery corn and lima beans that Aunt Joy called "succotash." Nyna took one bite then tried to hide the rest under her mashed potatoes. The gravy was grayish and pasty, which made Nyna miss Susan all the more. Susan made the best gravy in the world.

Nyna had to sit with Aunt Lois's little kids at a card table in the living room, and both of them—a five-year-old boy named Seamus and six-year-old girl named Joy Ann—had red hair and round, blue eyes that they crossed at Nyna through most of the dinner. Albert sat at the grown-up's table next to his dad, Uncle Al, a thick-armed, greasy- haired man with a big nose who kept telling Albert to sit up straight, swatting him lightly on the back of the head when he didn't do it right away.

Lorna sat on the other side of Albert, and Nyna watched her slide lima beans off her plate and into her hand, depositing them into the pocket of her dress. She'd started doing this at home with food she liked, saving it for later, but Nyna thought now she must be doing what Nyna herself was doing—trying to get rid of the weird stuff.

Kate Gadbow's stories and essays have appeared in *Epoch, Northwest Review, Cutbank, Talking River Review, The Montanan*, and elsewhere. She coedited the *Quill Reader*, published in 2000 by Harcourt Brace. Her novel *Pushed to Shore* was chosen by Rosellen Brown as winner of the 2001 Mary McCarthy Prize in Short Fiction and published by Sarabande Books of Louisville, Kentucky, in 2003. She directs the creative writing program and teaches undergraduate fiction classes at the University of Montana in Missoula, where she lives with her journalist husband, Daryl Gadbow.

2 tablespoons **olive oil**

4 ounces flaked **smoked salmon,**
all bones and skin removed

6 to 8 **shallots,** finely chopped

1 to 2 cloves **garlic,** pressed

1 6-ounce can of pitted **black olives,**
drained *(or really good black olives if
available)*

2 tablespoons **capers**

1 tablespoon **fresh basil,** chopped

2 to 3 medium-sized **tomatoes**

1 pound **fettuccine**

Freshly grated **Parmesan cheese**

Serves 4.

HUNGRY WOLF PASTA

*Working as a wolfwranglin' writer can make you hungrier than a pack of wolves. Usually
we only have time to slap together a burrito or heat up leftover spaghetti. But when time
allows, we enjoy preparing a special meal, and this is one of them. A friend of ours, who has
worked in five-star restaurants, passed this recipe on to us (so it must be good). This is the
kind of dinner that you can serve with a salad and then sit back and slowly eat while brain-
storming creative ideas or trying to sound like you're one of the literati.*

1. Bring a large pot of salted water to a boil—this is where you'll dump the fettuccine.

2. Heat the olive oil in a large skillet until the oil is hot enough to sauté the salmon,
shallots, garlic, olives, capers, and basil. Sauté until the shallots become translucent,
which should take about 5 minutes.

3. Meanwhile, back at the pot of boiling water, add the fettuccine and cook.

4. Return your attention to the skillet and add the tomatoes and sauté for a few more
minutes until the tomatoes are warmed all the way through.

5. Drain the pasta, add it to the skillet, and toss with the salmon mixture. Divide the
results of your labor among 4 heated plates and sprinkle with Parmesan cheese. At the
table, provide the peppermill and more grated Parmesan cheese for those who want it.
Then wolf it down.

From *Tales of Two Canines: The True Adventures of a Wolf and Dog*, from the chapter "Another Free Lunch" by Koani, the Wild Sentry Ambassador Wolf.

We had Big Excitement this week! Last Tuesday we headed out on a walk late in the afternoon like we always do. We'd gone about a quarter mile and crossed an irrigation ditch when I smelled something in a thicket of fir trees. Sniff, sniff, sniff, and then I plunged in, pulling Pat unceremoniously with me (for some reason she never wants to go into thick brush—no sense of adventure, I guess).

Suddenly, I spotted treasure—a dead deer, but so fresh that flies hadn't even found it. Only the innards and a little bit of the hindquarter were gone. Sticks and pine needles covered the carcass. Then I picked up a smell that made the hair on the back of my neck stand up. Mountain lion! I know Pat realized that a lion killed the deer because she started yelling for Indy as she looked up in the trees. Of course, he didn't pay any attention to Pat. He's convinced he can whip any cat there is.

She tried to pull me away from the deer carcass. NO WAY! I'm not stupid—I know cougars can be dangerous, especially when you're thieving from one of their kills. But I figured that if I could get away with it, this was free meat. So I stood there with my hackles up, looking all around. I grabbed a leg and pulled the deer towards a clearing.

A twig snapped! I jumped straight up in the air and surveyed the area with hyper-alert attention. When Pat saw me jump, she jumped and whirled around too. Then she laughed because she realized that I caused that twig to snap when I stepped on it. I calmed down and went back to work on the deer. Finally, I tugged it out in the open, and we all felt better. I settled down to eat. The cougar had left the very best part: the antlers, which were still in velvet.

Yummy! I crunched every last bit of them. Then I ate some meat, but I wasn't really very hungry, so we left. Of course, I put out signs that say, "This is Koani's Meat. Disturb at Your Own Risk." I do that by urinating. Then I scratched with my front feet so that big clods of grass and dirt flew behind me.

However, my warning didn't do much good. The next day, the deer was half gone. Four days later, we found only three lower legs. I'm not certain if it was the cougar that returned, but the deer definitely didn't go to waste.

I think I'd better sign off for now. Pat and Bruce are packing the van, so we're headed out on another trip. Muzzle Nuzzles, Koani.

Bruce Weide and **Pat Tucker** have directed Wild Sentry: The Northern Rockies Ambassador Wolf Program, a nonprofit environmental education program to promote a better understanding of wolves and wildlands. They have collaborated on two books, *There's a Wolf in the Classroom!* and *Tales of Two Canines: The True Adventures of a Wolf and Dog*, as well as the booklet *Can You Turn a Wolf into a Dog?* In addition, they have consulted on or appeared in numerous documentaries, including the *Wolves of the World* (BBC), *Wolves* (Discovery Channel's Animal Planet), and *Secret Life of Wolves* (Audubon/Disney).

Bruce has produced two award-winning documentaries, *The Wolf: Real or Imagined* (broadcast on PBS) and *Was That A Wolf?* He holds a BA in geography and an MFA in creative writing from the University of Montana. Pat received a BA in nursing from California State University—Chico and earned her MS in wildlife biology from the University of Montana.

You can visit the Wild Sentry website at www.wildsentry.org.

PUTTANESCA

This so-called "harlot" sauce —puttanesca is Italian for "lady of the evening"—was quick and easy to make, and was, legend has it, enjoyed with the last client of the night.

○ ○

Good **olive oil**

2 or 3 cloves **garlic**

4 flat **anchovy filets**

1 large can *(28 ounces)* **tomatoes,** chopped or 3 or so cups of fresh garden tomatoes

1 cup oil-cured **olives,** pitted and coarsely chopped

2 tablespoons **capers**

$\frac{1}{4}$ teaspoon hot **red pepper**

3 to 4 tablespoons **pine nuts**

1 cup grated **peccorino romano cheese**

1 pound **rigatoni**

Serves 4.

1. Start water for rigatoni.

2. Cover the bottom of a large frying pan with olive oil and heat. Cook garlic and anchovies gently in the oil.

3. Add tomatoes, olives, and capers. Simmer sauce for 15 or 20 minutes. Anchovies will dissolve.

4. Cook rigatoni.

5. Serve the rigatoni with a generous portion of puttanesca on top. Just before serving sauce, add pine nuts and romano cheese and stir in. My favorite accompaniments are sweet barbecued Italian sausage, crusty Italian or French bread, and good red wine.

Try your own modifications. Chopped fresh basil or Italian parsley are great additions. Some insist this dish wasn't served with cheese, so if that suits, try it without.

From "Think Global, Eat Local," published in the *Los Angeles Times Magazine*, July 2005.

Greg Higgins, chef and owner of the tony downtown Portland restaurant Higgins, walks to the back of his bustling kitchen and opens the heart of the latest environmental movement, the walk-in refrigerator. It is crammed with sides of beef covered with blankets of fat, glassy-eyed fish, rows of restaurant-made sausage and ham, trays of fresh vegetables in plastic tubs and other assorted comestibles, nearly all of it originating within a hundred miles of here, in what Higgins calls the Portland "foodshed." Virtually every item is brought in and dropped off by the farmer who raised it. "There's nothing more threatened than the American farmer," says the tall, burly Higgins a little later, as he swirls and sips from a glass of white wine. "The goal is to keep them in business."

A personal connection between a restaurant chef and the family who grows the beef or broccoli rabe might not sound radical, but it's a major element of a burgeoning movement. It's called "sustainable food" and sustainable means that it's done in a way in which the practice can go on in perpetuity. It accomplishes a number of goals: it cuts down on oil consumption, puts money in the pockets of disappearing farmers, is more humane, helps protect soil and water and, not least of all, usually tastes better.

That this kind of relationship is even news is an indication of how crazy the food production and distribution system has become. Food is no longer an artisanal process, but a commodity. Large food producers focus on making products as cheaply as possible, and consumers are waking up to the fact that something's wrong. Things are getting weird out there in Hooterville: cloned cattle and sheep, genetically modified "Frankenfoods," schools of pen-raised and chemically dyed salmon, Mad Cow disease and E. coli in beef, mercury and PCBs in fish, chickens crammed into cages the size of a sheet of paper, and giant hog farms that pollute water sheds and raise a stink for miles around. Rivers of topsoil get washed away by large-scale farming and pesticides are released into the environment and wind up in human breast milk. Small farm and ranch families are disappearing, while large corporate farms reap huge federal subsidies. And it all floats on a sea of cheap diesel. The average American dinner travels 1,500 miles to get to the plate.

Jim Robbins is a regular contributor to the *New York Times* from his home in Helena. He is the author of *Last Refuge: Environmental Showdown in the American West* and *A Symphony in the Brain: The Evolution of the New Brainwave Biofeedback.* This year he will publish *The Art of Attending*, a book on the physiology and psychology of paying attention.

CHILES RELLENOS CASSEROLE

5 to 6 **poblano chiles,** the dark green Mexican chiles

1 cup **black beans,** or **pinto** or **Anasazi**

2 cups **brown rice**

2 or 3 **sausages,** preferably Uncle Bill's andouille, or any similar type, chopped and sautéed

1 to 2 tablespoon **oil** *(olive, peanut, or vegetable)*

2 to 3 hot **chile peppers** to taste, such as jalapeño, serrano, yellow wax, or red Fresno, chopped

1 small **onion,** chopped

2 cloves **garlic,** minced

$\frac{1}{2}$ pound **Monterey** or **Pepper Jack cheese,** cut into strips

1 cup grated **cheddar cheese**

3 **eggs**

$\frac{1}{4}$ cup **flour**

$\frac{3}{4}$ cup **milk**

Serves 4.

1. Scorch, peel, and remove the seeds and stems from 5 or 6 poblanos, the dark green Mexican chiles. The idea is to come up with approximately 6 peeled chiles, but the size of the chiles varies and this can reduce the number to 4 or 5. It also depends on the size of the dish used for baking. I use a familiar Corningware 2-quart casserole dish. The peppers may be prepared well in advance and kept refrigerated for a day or so.

2. Cook the black beans and reserve at least 1 cup for the casserole. If you feel compelled to use canned beans, be sure to rinse and drain to get rid of all that sugar and gluey extraneous stuff.

3. Cook the brown rice and reserve at least 2 cups for the casserole.

4. Preheat oven to 350°.

5. In a large frying pan, sauté the chopped sausage in a reasonable amount of oil. Add the chopped peppers and cook for a minute or two before adding the chopped onion and minced garlic, cook until soft. Combine this sausage, pepper, onion, and garlic mixture with the beans and rice in a large bowl.

6. Grease or butter the casserole dish. Stuff each poblano with the sausage/rice/bean mixture and place in the casserole dish with the poblanos more or less reformed as close to their original shape as you can, with the slit side up.

7. Into each poblano put a strip or two of the jack cheese and close. The poblanos may be arranged in rows, side by side, or any way that seems to adequately fill the available space. Sprinkle the grated cheddar cheese over everything.

8. Beat the eggs with the flour until smooth. Add the milk and blend well. Pour this over the stuffed poblanos.

9. Bake, uncovered, for 45 minutes, or until the top is very crusty and brown. Check at 35 minutes. Altitude can play a part in length of cooking. It could take an hour. Remove from oven and let the casserole sit for 10 minutes or so before cutting with a sharp knife and serving with a large spoon.

The whole thing comes to something like 1,200 calories. A wedge ($\frac{1}{8}$) would run approximately 150 calories, or less.

BROCCOLI, GARBANZO BEAN, and ALMOND ENCHILADAS

Notes on Food:

I quit eating meat when I moved away from home after high school. Many of my older relatives believed that I would soon be dead from malnutrition. But the opposite happened. I tended to be sick less, although it's impossible to say if it was my diet that did it. It could have been moving away from home. Or it could have been leaving Arizona and living instead in Oregon. What else happened when I went away to college? I got a girlfriend. That was great. And, for the first time, I was in a place where people took seriously reading and writing and thinking. People wanted to talk about ideas.

For whatever reason, my health improved. I felt that I was lighter and quicker and, at the same time, that I had more strength and endurance. My basketball game improved though I still turned my right ankle too often.

The wrapping:
24 **corn tortillas**

The filling:

1 medium **onion,** finely chopped

3 or 4 **Anaheim chiles,** chopped

1 **jalapeño pepper,** chopped

$\frac{1}{2}$ **red sweet pepper,** chopped

$\frac{1}{2}$ **yellow sweet pepper,** chopped

1 or 2 stems and flowerets of fresh **broccoli**

1 cup **raw whole almonds**

Fresh **cilantro,** to taste *(save some for the topping)*

$1\frac{1}{2}$ cups cooked **garbanzo beans** *(if canned, rinse well)*

Mild **cheese,** to taste

The wrapping and filling:

1. Put $\frac{3}{4}$ to 1 inch of oil in a frying pan slightly larger than the diameter of the tortillas. Heat the oil as hot as it can get before smoking—canola oil is good because it can take a lot of heat before it burns—and put a tortilla in the oil, making sure it's fully immersed, then turn it over and fry for a few seconds longer, keeping the tortilla moving. The entire process should take 10 to 15 seconds and the finished tortilla should still be flexible.

2. Remove the tortilla from the oil and let the excess oil drip off. Put the tortilla on a plate and cover it with an uncooked tortilla. Repeated until you have cooked 24 tortillas. Once the tortillas are cooked, set them aside.

3. Fry the onion in some of the tortilla oil until translucent. Remove the onion and put it in a large bowl.

4. Fry the chilies and peppers together, also using the tortilla oil. Put them in the bowl with the onion.

David Romtvedt

The sauce:
1 dozen fresh **tomatillos**

¾ cup **orange juice**

¼ cup **red wine**

3 heaping tablespoons mild **red chili powder**

1 heaping tablespoon **cumin**

½ teaspoon **cardamom**

½ teaspoon **cinnamon**

1 tablespoon **creamy peanut butter**

1 ounce **semisweet baking chocolate** or 2 teaspoons cocoa powder

Grated peel of 1 **orange**

3 to 4 tablespoons **arrowroot powder** (or cornstarch)

½ cup of cold **water**

The topping:
¾ cup **nonfat yogurt**

¾ cup high fat **sour cream**

2 **avocados**, peeled and sliced

Serves 6.

5. Fry the broccoli in the same manner and put in the bowl.

6. Chop almonds, roast them in a dry pan, and add them to the other ingredients.

7. Add cilantro. If you have an anti-cilantro person coming to dinner (some people say cilantro tastes like soap), leave it out.

8. Add garbanzo beans and cheese. How much cheese? As much as you like. My Kenyan friend John Kambutu once asked me, "What's with Americans and cheese?"

The sauce:
1. To make the sauce, blend the tomatillos until they are liquid—don't mind the seeds. Put them in a 2-quart saucepan and add orange juice, wine, and enough water to make 5 cups of liquid. Add the remaining ingredients except the arrowroot and mix well.

2. Stir the arrowroot powder into cold water. When smooth, add it to the sauce and turn the heat up to medium low. Stir continually for 5 to 10 minutes until the sauce thickens. It'll take on a lovely shiny gloss. If it's not thickening, mix a little more arrowroot into cold water and add it, but stir continually. When the sauce has thickened, remove it from the heat.

3. Pour some of the sauce into the filling mix and stir until everything is thoroughly mixed. Spread sauce on the bottom and sides of two casseroles. Put a little sauce on a small plate and put a tortilla down on the plate. Turn the tortilla so that both sides are covered lightly with the sauce. Put a mound of the filling on the gooey tortilla and roll it up.

4. Lay the rolled tortillas side by side in the casseroles. This is the best part—it's a mess, sauce all over your hands, and every time you put your gooey hands on the spoon to get more sauce out of the pan the mess gets bigger. Oh, well. Keep filling tortillas until you have 12 in each casserole. If there is any sauce left, you can spread it over the top of the tortillas or save it for some other concoction. Spread grated cheese over the top of the filled casseroles. Bake covered in a 375° oven for 20 minutes. Remove the covering and bake for another 5 to 10 minutes.

The topping:

1. Mix the sour cream and yogurt together till smooth. When you serve the enchiladas, spoon some of the yogurt/sour cream mixture over each portion. Put sliced avocados and chopped cilantro on top and eat.

○ ○

From the forthcoming *Some Church*, to be published in fall 2005 by Milkweed Editions.

Plums

Here in Wyoming it is possible to grow plums but barely.
My trees stand twisted and short, the wind heaving at them
and the snow piling up in drifts along the south wall
where in summer the heat might let blossoms turn to fruit.

I planted a final tree beside the deck
so that when I sit the light comes dappled down
through the leaves and litters the pages of my book,
pools of light and dark through which I go on reading.

Once in twenty years we've had plums, small and hard
then slowly growing larger, the matte dusting of blue
almost like the sky. It's not so much that I wanted
to eat the plums but to have them meant something more.

And so I went on reading and thinking about what purpose
any of us has beyond the moment in which we sit or stand,
roll our shoulders and shake our hair, hop on one leg
just to know we can and then laugh or shout at a crow.

The afternoon went on and the light came longer, beams
drawn out, somehow hotter than earlier in the day. I turned
and reached toward the tree, pulled a plum off and ate it,
and the flesh was warm and yellow and not too firm.

○ ○ ○ ○ ○ ○ ○ ○ ○ ○ ○ ○ ○ ○ ○ ○ ○ ○ ○

David Romtvedt is a writer and musician. His books of poetry include *Certainty*, *How Many Horses*, and *A Flower Whose Name I Do Not Know* (a selection of the National Poetry Series). He has also published the fictional history *Crossing Wyoming* and a nonfiction collection, *Windmill: Essays from Four Mile Ranch*. His newest book of poetry, *Some Church*, was published by Milkweed Editions in fall 2005. Though he lives in Buffalo, Wyoming, and serves as that state's poet laureate, he spent many years working in the Montana Writers-in-the-Schools program and is aware that for many people Wyoming is Montana's southernmost county.

Marnie Prange

1½ pounds **beef round,**
cut in 2-inch pieces

Flour

Salt and **pepper**

Cayenne pepper

2 tablespoons **oil,** or **lard** laced
with bacon fat

1 tablespoon **garlic,** minced

1 cup **onion,** chopped

1 ripe **tomato,** chopped

1 cup **water**

Grits or **cheese grits**

Serves 4.

GRITS and GRILLADES

This is the first recipe I served in Montana, back in 1987. Everyone enjoyed eating this Cajun fare, especially Jim Welch, who liked the novelty of grits.

1. Pound beef pieces with a meat mallet until doubled in size.

2. Dredge with seasoned flour, salt, pepper, and cayenne pepper.

3. Brown in oil or lard laced with bacon fat.

4. Add garlic, onion, and tomato to browned meat.

5. Pour in 1 cup of water, cover loosely, and simmer over low heat for 30 minutes, turning meat every 10 minutes. If gravy gets too thick, add water.

6. Serve over grits or cheese grits.

SLUMGULLION (for John States)

A single blade

Swiss Army Knife

bought cheap

Army-Navy store

Higgin's Ave Missoula

a potato

a cold handle sheet steel

fry pan Woods Second

Hand on Alder

a bunch of green onions

half a zucchini

a chunk of butter

throw all this together

using the knife

to chop it turn

the heat low

'til the spuds

are tender

then a half pound

of burger will go

nicely in the pan

crumbled in chunks

turn the heat

up a notch put back

your lid sip a beer

read a line or two

the burger

should steam up fast

then you've got a juicy

mess into which

throw two or three

eggs and stir

find a plate

and a fork

sit down

if you've got a table

and chair

and make your

growling gut

happy

add: salt

pepper catsup

or whatever

hot sauce you

got guts for

David Thomas's most recent book is *The Hellgate Wind*. He is also the author of *Buck's Last Wreck* and *Fossil Fuel*. He has poems included in *The Last Best Place*. He lives and works in Missoula, Montana.

Earl Ganz

4 ounces of **flat noodles**

1 tablespoon **butter** or **margarine**

2 large **zucchinis**

1 pound of your favorite **Monterey Jack cheese.**

ZUCCHINI DELIGHT

1. Put the noodles in eight cups of boiling water.

2. When they are almost done, melt a tablespoon of butter or margarine in a 12-inch nonstick fry pan.

3. Slice two large zucchinis into rounds about a $\frac{1}{4}$-inch thick. Spread them flat in the pan and sauté them on medium heat for about 2 minutes or until they are beginning to brown on one side.

4. While they are browning, slice the pound of Monterey Jack into $\frac{1}{4}$-inch-thick slices.

5. Drain the noodles into a colander. Turn the heat under the fry pan to a simmer and pour the noodles over the zucchini. Mix them, then level them and place the slices of cheese over the mix. Turn the heat off. Cover the pan and let the heat from the noodles, zucchini, and the pan itself melt the cheese slices.

6. You're done.

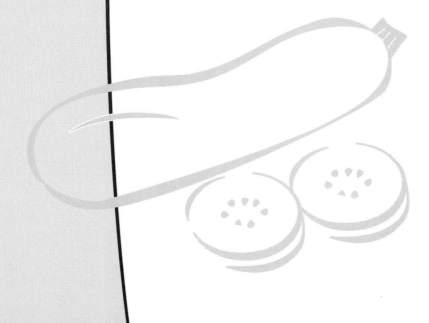

From *The Truth Game*, forthcoming from the University of New Mexico Press in January 2006.

They started with sizzling rice soup. As much as for its taste, they loved the ceremony.

The waiter would deliver a tureen of steaming shrimp broth to the tray stand, then, with a flourish, uncover a steel serving dish to reveal the crenulated clusters of rice.

He'd let their smoke rise a moment, then, with metal serving tongs, grab two or three of the clusters, flourish them in the air, finally placing them in the broth where they would go off like small fire-crackers on a Chinese New Year. During the winter of 1938, Myron had brought Tony here and they always ordered this dish. So it was Tony who first pointed it out. China man look like Mabel, he said. And Myron saw what Tony meant. It was Mabel when she was burning pine boughs to drive out the stale air. Even now as he watched the waiter, he could see Mabel doing her little dance.

It's so stuffy in here! she would say as she ran from one corner of the room to another waving the crackling pinon boughs. It's so stuffy!

But here in Sing Wu's it wasn't stuffy, and the aroma wasn't pinon. It was onion, garlic, and shrimp. Myron looked around. The nearby diners were staring wide-eyed.

The waiter had finished filling the tureen, but the rice was still popping. When it was quiet the man began ladling the soup into two small bowls and the people at the other tables broke into applause. The waiter nodded, put a bowl in front of Myron, then Steve, then left and everyone turned to their food except Myron.

He was looking at his friend. His young lover, nearly seventy now, was still a handsome man. His birthday was coming up soon . What can I get him? Myron wondered. Thirty-two years we've been together. It had been good time. Then he thought of a gift. They'd talked about it before. And Steve had a nephew who knew about such things. I'll call him in the morning. Yes, a computer, and Myron nodded at his decision. Then he lifted his ceramic spoon and filled his mouth with warm pleasure.

Born in Brooklyn in 1932, **Earl Ganz** came to Missoula in 1966 to teach in the English department and head the new MFA program in creative writing. He retired in 1996. One of the great things that happened to him in Montana was that he got to know Myron Brinig, a once famous novelist from Butte who died in 1991 at the age of ninety-four. In 2001, while living in Albuquerque, Ganz began a novel about Brinig, which the University of New Mexico Press will release in January 2006. Ganz lives with his wife, Karen, in Lake Charles, Louisiana.

MONTANA WINTER CASSEROLE

Wade through snow, brush off the truck, slide on icy highways until you reach the grocery store. Leave the car running with the heater on full blast and the windshield wipers slapping away snowflakes. On your way into the store, stop 11 times to greet neighbors who also hit town on such a crummy day. Share your recipe with everybody in the place, find out who's pregnant and who sold their grampa's section of land to developers, admire the storekeeper's new heeler puppy, and hear about Mrs. So-and-So's daughter's scholarship. Then buy some fresh vegetables, a lottery ticket, a can of snoose for the old man, and head home.

1 layer sliced raw **potatoes** (*these are from your root cellar, saved from the crop that didn't get enough water because you were camping at Canyon Ferry that dry weekend*)

1 layer **onions,** chopped (*maybe a Walla-Walla from your neighbor in exchange for the barn cat you gave her*)

1 cup each, **celery** and **green pepper,** chopped

2 pounds of good Montana **ground beef,** cooked and drained

1 large can of **tomatoes**

Season with 2 tablespoons **oil,** 3 tablespoons **brown sugar** plus a pinch of **salt, pepper,** and **oregano.**

(*I'll bet you thought you could get through a Montana woman's recipe without reading the word "pinch." Well, you were wrong...*)

Serves 4.

1. Mix ingredients together in a 9-inch by 13-inch pan.

2. Bake for 2 hours in a 350° oven while you're playing gin rummy at the kitchen table with Uncle Ned, Aunt Hazel, and Carl, your neighbor who stopped in to borrow jumper cables.

3. While you're eating, another neighbor drops in, greeting you with that most famous of Montana phrases heard from September through May: "Cold enough for you?"

From *Beyond Proud Shores*, forthcoming from Manchester Publishing in March 2007.

1840
New England

The ship's stench, putrid and sour, carried ashore on the biting wind, announcing its approach before the vessel reached port. Weather-beaten sails held hostage for too long by the ceaseless wind clattered in protest, and blackened hull timbers groaned in agony as The Scollard lumbered into the harbor.

Its rag-tag crew had not seen home for nearly two years. Now, the disparate rabble gathered on deck: West Indians, Portuguese, Azorean and American sailors, whalers all. Scrawny, sun-leathered and exhausted, their collective shouts joined the cacophony of lapping waves, screeching gulls and the footfall of children clambering down the pier to greet the ship.

There was little excitement that rivaled the return of a whaling ship to the village. Children knew that after the cargo was unloaded—barrels of blubber- rendered oil, wooden casks of pure, waxy spermaceti, and crates of baleen—the sailors would swagger through the hoards, dispensing handiwork they'd created during prolonged periods of inactivity at sea or acquired in exotic ports.

"Had ya' a good run, man?" Charles Cushman stood aside from the frenetic crowd of youngsters, hollering above the wind to catch the second mate's attention. An underwriter of the voyage, Cushman had a vested interest in the cargo; the crew's welfare was of little concern to him, save their ability to bring home a cash crop.

"A fine run, sir," Elliot Martin called above the din. He angled toward the banker, leaning into the wind, but stopped short at a civilized distance. The smell of whale flensing and months-old sweat could be excused by another sailor, but not by those on land. "I'll wager there's enough baleen in those crates to supply carriage springs to every village on the coast. And oil a'plenty. Indeed, it was a fine run."

"Mind yourself in port," Cushman admonished the sailor. No good came from the whalers when they hit the harbortown taverns.

Lauri Olsen wrote for magazines and newspapers before turning her energy toward books. Her three young-adult novels are *Big Sky Dreams, Cold Moon Honor, and Dancer in the Mist* (Avalon, New York). Her fourth book, *Whispers on the Wind: Stories of Women from Montana's Past* (Timberline Press, Spokane), was her first non-fiction work. Her fifth book, *Pacific Bound* (Gossamer Books, San Francisco), is a children's graphic novel based on the Lewis and Clark journey and was written to help children with dyslexia who cannot focus on traditional history books.

CHINESE HOT DISH

In addition to my television show, Today in Montana, *I also assisted Maxine Otis, home service advisor for the Great Falls Gas Company, on her biweekly cooking show,* Hospitality Time, *that immediately followed my television show from 9:00 to 9:30 a.m.*

We had a kitchen set up in the studio and Maxine prepared dishes on the air. We offered the recipes to our viewers and the response was overwhelming.

The Great Falls Gas Company published a cookbook featuring 185 of the favorite recipes demonstrated on Hospitality Time, *which was broadcast on KRTV for more than 6 years. At the time it was the longest running television program in Montana that was presented with a single sponsor.*

Of all the recipes Maxine shared, my favorite from her cookbook, long out of print, is Chinese Hot Dish, one that has become a tradition in our family. We serve it regularly, especially on Christmas Eve.

1 pound **ground beef**

2 tablespoons **fat**

1 cup **onion,** finely chopped

$\frac{1}{2}$ cup uncooked **rice**

1 can **chicken rice soup**

1 soup can of **water**

4 tablespoons **soy sauce**

1 cup **celery,** finely diced

Half a package frozen **peas**

Serves 4.

1. Brown meat in fat.

2. Add chopped onion and cook until golden and transparent.

3. Add rice, soup, water, and soy sauce.

4. Place in 2-quart covered casserole and bake in 400° oven for 1 hour.

5. During the last 20 minutes, add celery and frozen peas. More liquid may be needed.

From *Movie Stars & Rattlesnakes*, published by Farcountry Press in 2004.

That afternoon, Paul Harvey entered the Cascade High School playing field to an estimated crowd of 3,000 men, women, and children. The crowds sat on bleachers and on the grass.

Each of these people paid $7.50 a ticket, which admitted them to the speech as well as to a beef barbeque afterward. Nine area ranchers donated the beef. The steaks and hamburgers were grilled on a 75-foot-long grill, which was constructed on cinderblocks. Potatoes were cooked over coals in a giant pit that was dug. Large plastic bags full of homemade salad were dished up, along with rolls and beverages. It was a feast.

People had come from everywhere in Montana and the nation, especially those who had once lived in Cascade. It far surpassed the town's expectations and the Corneliuses were repaid. After expenses, the profits were between $12,000 and $14,000, which were given to the library and the Senior Citizens' Center.

Norma Ashby of Great Falls, author of *Movie Stars & Rattlesnakes: The Heyday of Montana Live Television*, is a fourth-generation Montanan. Born and raised in Helena, she graduated from the University of Montana in Missoula in journalism and worked three summers as a reporter for the *Helena Independent Record*. After working 4 years in the magazine field in New York City, she returned to Great Falls in 1961, where she has lived ever since.

Norma was a broadcaster with KRTV for 26 years. As hostess and producer of the award-winning *Today in Montana* show, she interviewed more than 26,000 people. She wrote and produced 21 television documentaries and coauthored *Symbols of Montana*.

Norma's new book, released by Farcountry Press in 2004, is the story of Norma's career in broadcasting. In the course of 7,000 shows, she talked to seven Montana governors and first ladies, and people ranging from movie star Clint Eastwood to rattlesnake handler Cyril Colarcheck.

She has been married to Shirley Ashby, a retired banker and native of Helena, since 1964. They have two children, Ann and Tony, and three grandsons, Bill, Jack, and Dusty.

James Lee Burke

$\frac{1}{2}$ to 1 stick **butter**
(or $\frac{1}{4}$ cup light olive oil)

2 medium **onions**

1 stalk **celery**

1 **green pepper**

1 clove **garlic**

1 pound **crawfish tails**

1 cup **chicken broth** (or water)

Salt and **pepper,** to taste

Dash of **cayenne pepper** to taste

1 tablespoon **cornstarch** (or flour)

1 **green onion,** chopped

Serves 4.

CRAWFISH ETOUFEE

1. Mince the onions, celery, green pepper, and garlic. Simmer vegetables in melted butter for 15 minutes until onions are clear and vegetables are soft.

2. Add crawfish, broth, and seasoning. Bring to a boil. Turn down heat and simmer for 15 minutes. Add more broth if needed.

3. Dissolve cornstarch in a small amount of water, then add slowly. Stir and cook until thickened.

4. Add green onion tops, stir, and serve over cooked rice.

From *Purple Cane Road*, published by Dell Publishing Company in August 2001.

This excerpt introduces the reader to the bait shop and boat rental run by the fictional police officer Dave Robicheaux.

On Saturday I woke early, before sunrise, to help Batist, the elderly black man who worked for me, open the bait shop and fire the barbecue pit on which we prepared chickens and links for our mid-day customers. I unhooked Tripod, Alafair's pet three-legged coon, from his chain and set him on top of the rabbit hutch with a bowl of water and a bowl of fish scraps. But he hopped down on the ground and walked ahead of me through the pecan and oak trees and across the dirt road to the dock, his tail and rear end swaying.

He and Batist had been at war for years, Tripod flinging boudin all over the counter, destroying boxes of fried pies and candy bars, Batist chasing him down the dock with a broom, threatening to cook him in a pot. But finally they had declared a truce, either out of their growing age or their recognition of their mutual intractability. Now, whenever Alafair or I turned Tripod loose, he usually headed for the dock and worked the screen open and slept on top of the icebox behind the counter. Last week I saw Batist roaring down the bayou in an outboard, with Tripod sitting on the bow, his face pointed in to the breeze like a hood ornament.

James Lee Burke was born in 1936 in Houston, Texas, and grew up on the Louisiana-Texas coast. He attended Southwestern Louisiana Institute (now the University of Louisiana at Lafayette), and later the University of Missouri at Columbia, where he received an BA and MA in English literature.

Over the years, he has worked as a pipeliner, land surveyor, social worker, newspaper reporter, and U.S. Forest Service employee. He has also taught at the University of Missouri, University of Southwestern Louisiana, University of Montana, Miami-Dade Community College, and Wichita State University. Over the years he has published 24 novels and 1 collection of short stories. Two novels, *Heaven's Prisoners* and *Two for Texas*, were adapted as motion pictures. Mr. Burke's work has received two Edgar Awards for best crime novel of the year. He is also a Bread Loaf fellow and Guggenheim fellow and was the recipient of an NEA grant.

He and his wife of 45 years, Pearl Burke, who is originally from Mainland China, have four children and divide their time between Missoula, Montana, and New Iberia, Louisiana.

CATFISH WILEY

Invented by DQ, a simplistic but exuberant cook; named in honor of his much-beloved step-dog, Wiley Gaines Q. The guiding principles of this recipe are that a) catfish is low on the food chain, therefore a good staple protein, yet can be tasty; b) catfish is too bland and subtle to countenance garlic; c) zucchini also is bland and subtle; d) there is no such thing, in the face of bland subtlety, as too much black pepper.

○ ○

1 quarter-inch knuckle of **ginger**

2 to 3 tablespoons **olive oil**

3 medium **zucchinis**

1 **egg**

2 medium filets of **catfish**

　Salt and coarse-ground **black pepper**

　Fine **bread crumbs**

　Olive oil as needed

　Salt

1 cup **white wine**

　Half a **lemon**

　Basmati rice

　Serves 2.

1. Dice the ginger and begin sizzling in olive oil in a sauté pan. Slice the zucchinis longitudinally in half, then slice again diagonally every $\frac{1}{4}$-inch or so, to yield a whole bunch of half-oval pieces, easily sautéed. Get them frizzing gently with the ginger; cover pan.

2. Make a Bombay martini, dry, on the rocks, and put it in the freezer.

3. Beat the egg in a bowl and slime the catfish filets in it. Dust the filets lightly with salt and liberally with black pepper, on both eggy sides. Then dredge seasoned filets through the bread crumbs. Seasoning the filets before breading them gets the pepper in deep.

4. Start the rice cooking. One cup dry rice per person, if you're hungry. Set your wrist alarm for 18 minutes; cover.

5. In an old grumpy black cast-iron skillet, bring olive oil to medium-high. Lay in the catfish filets as the heat is coming up. Turn the heat to medium (all of this on a gas stove, of course, so changes happen promptly). Give them a good 2- to 3-minute browning on side 1, flip delicately to side 2, brown again 2 to 3 minutes. Turn heat to low.

6. Pull out the martini and begin drinking it. *Check the zucchini!* Stir it, salt it, pepper it generously, cover again.

7. When the catfish is browned, turn filets skin-side down (though the skin is gone, this puts the roughened rib-side on top), and add a cup or so of white wine. *Zzssshh!* Squeeze juice of half a lemon over the filets; pepper (liberally) and salt (modestly) them again. Scoop sautéed zucchini out of its pan with a slotted spoon and pile it over the catfish; splash in a little more white wine (what the hell) and cover the skillet.

8. Read a few pages of a good book while enjoying the martini. Turn off the rice after 18 minutes. Stir the rice. Turn off all the heat, uncover the catfish, let it breathe, set the table.

9. Pour glasses of good sauvignon blanc or champagne, not the rotgut chardonnay that went onto the fish.

10. Give your dog a deeply appreciative hug around the neck. He doesn't eat fish, but he's happy just to be with you.

11. Serve. Feeds your spouse and self.

From *Monster of God*, published by W. W. Norton & Company in 2003.

This describes a walking tour I made, in the Carpathian Mountains of Romania, in order to ask local shepherds about their attitudes toward brown bears.

With a venturous young translator named Ciprian ("Chip") Pavel, I set off on a series of hikes into the high country. We climb steep, wooded slopes above the mountain roads, above the trails, following hoofprints and sheep shit toward the alpine meadows where shepherds spend the summer. Sometimes we carry simple provisions (red-deer sausage, peanuts, raisins, chocolate) as well as sleeping bags and a tent. Sometimes we carry gifts (fresh oranges, cigarettes, pint bottles of a Romanian plum brandy called palinca) for the shepherds. Usually we carry walking sticks for defense against the dogs. We see some gorgeous landscape—mountain lakes, stony ridges and peaks, swales of verdant grass, fog-shrouded expanses of krummholz and heather, all of it chilly and wet even at the height of what, down in the lowlands, is a summer drought. We talk with dozens of nut-hard, gentle-spirited men. We're welcomed often with warm hospitality, candid comments, log seats beside a cook fire, hot mamaliga (Romanian polenta, grainy and yellow, served as a steaming paste) and freshly made cheese of the three traditional kinds: urda (sweet and crumbly), telemea (salty, like feta, but easily sliced), and branza de burduf (sweet and smooth, packed for market in cylinders sewn from fir bark). Rarely we face the cold truculence of a camp boss who wants no visitors and no palaver. Among the many things I discover is that this research regimen, so rich in exercise, cold mountain air, and cheese, may be bad for my cholesterol count but is highly agreeable to my disposition.

David Quammen is a two-time recipient of the National Magazine Award for his science essays and other work in *Outside* magazine. His newest work is *Monster of God: The Man-Eating Predator in the Jungles of History and the Mind.* His books include *The Boilerplate Rhino: Nature in the Eye of the Beholder* and *The Song of the Dodo: Island Biogeography in an Age of Extinction.* He lives in Bozeman.

Fred Haefele

⅓ cup plus 2 tablespoons **olive oil**

½ cup **onion,** finely chopped

½ cup **celery,** finely chopped

1 pound fresh **tomato,** peeled chopped

2 tablespoons **tomato sauce**

1 cup dry **white wine**

¾ cup **parsley**

1 **bay leaf,** crumbled

Salt and **pepper**

3 cloves **garlic,** minced

1 pound **shelled shrimp**

½ pound **feta cheese,** crumbled

2 tablespoons **ouzo**

Cooked **orzo**

Feeds 4 hungry treemen.

SHRIMP with FETA

1. Heat ⅓ cup oil in skillet, sauté onions and celery, add tomatoes and tomato sauce. Stirring constantly, bring mixture to a boil, then cover and reduce heat. Simmer 10 minutes.

2. Stir in white wine, parsley, bay leaf, salt, and pepper and simmer 30 minutes.

3. Heat 2 tablespoons oil in large skillet and sauté garlic and shrimp until the shrimp turn light pink.

4. Pour part of the sauce in baking dish and submerge shrimp therein. Sprinkle with half of the feta. Add remainder of sauce and sprinkle with remaining feta. Bake for 20 minutes at 350°.

5. Garnish with ouzo and parsley. Serve with cooked orzo.

From *Rebuilding the Indian*, published by Riverhead Books in 1998.

The plan is to paddle hard, get as far as we can before we put in for the night. The autumn light reflecting off the river is magnificent, startlingly clear. The cottonwoods are bare, the bench land is buff-colored, the river green, powerful and fast. I'm in the bow, Peter is in the stern. With each stroke, the temperature seems to drop, and I understand that inside an hour or two, our situation could be serious, and that it will require all the attention and carefulness we can muster.

Around every bend, great flights of waterfowl rise before us by the thousands: mallards and wigeons, wood ducks and teal, Canada and snow geese, all driven down river by the arctic front.

At the very end of the light, with the temperatures still dropping, we finally head for shore, where Peter and I make camp with a quiet urgency. There's plenty of deadwood scattered around, so I abandon the Coleman, go with an open fire and a folding grate, cook our pasta puttanesca. We eat quickly, then scour the cottonwood groves, build the fire up, then settle in close for Oreos and whiskey. Coincidentally, Peter and I both wear brand new forest green wool pants with razor creases, which give the bivouac a goofy kind of elegance. With the flashlight on Peter's thermometer, we see its five degrees, and it seems like an accomplishment, just pitching the tent and feeding ourselves...."

Fred Haefele received his MFA from the University of Montana in 1981. His essays have appeared in *American Heritage, Outside,* the *New York Times Magazine, Wired,* and other publications. He has received literary fellowships from The Fine Arts Work Center, the NEA, and Stanford University. He is the author of the motorcycle memoir *Rebuilding the Indian,* published by Riverhead Books in1998 and reprinted by Bison Books in 2005. A certified arborist, Haefele currently lives in Missoula with his wife and two children.

TROUT and MORELS

Eat it all or share it with two or three others.

○ ○

A big **trout**, 1 to 3 pounds

A bunch of **morel mushrooms**, sliced if large

White wine **salad dressing** *(such as Girard's Champagne dressing)*

Rice, as much as you want

Half an **onion**

1 or 2 cloves **garlic**

1 to 2 tablespoons **olive oil**

1 tablespoon **butter**

Splash of **sherry**

Salt and **pepper**

Serves 4.

1. Catch and kill a big trout (or buy some salmon if you're squeamish about killing trout).

2. Gather a bunch of morels under cottonwoods by the river in May and June or from recent burns in July.

3. Cut the filets from the trout, removing the ribs but leaving the skin, and marinate them in white wine dressing overnight in the fridge.

4. Cook the rice sometime before or during the following process.

5. Go outside and preheat a gas or charcoal grill.

6. Go inside and cut up the onion, garlic, and the morels (if they're big ones).

7. Cover the bottom of a sauté pan with olive oil and put it on medium heat for 5 minutes. Put in the garlic and onions. Sauté for 10 minutes or so.

8. Add the morels, butter, a splash of sherry, and a sprinkle of salt and/or pepper.

9. Go outside to the grill and put the trout on the grill, skin-side down.

10. Go back in and smell the mushrooms for 10 to 15 minutes, then turn them and add another splash of sherry.

11. Go back out to the grill and turn the trout onto the meat side, just long enough to sear the flesh.

12. Run back in and add more salt, pepper, butter, and sherry to the pan.

13. Nuke the rice if you cooked it earlier and put it on a platter.

14. Run out, take trout off the grill, and place meat-side down on the rice. Remove the skin.

15. Run back in and put the mushrooms and sauce on the trout and rice.

In The Who's Who of the River

If you gather morels by a river, then
They'll taste like that river. If you eat the morels
With trout, they won't be redundant. But then again....
Spring evenings I've watched the deer move themselves
Along the margins of cottonwood groves. And mornings
I've noticed the nibbled stalks of morels. I must
Have a word with these deer, perhaps of warning,
Perhaps of advice. But what would it be? Trust?
Share? Shoo? In the who's who of the river,
I'm afraid I'm rather low on the totem pole.
If you eat morels with deer, you'll never
Hear the end of it. You'll have swallowed a whole
Lexicon. You'll be a walking refrain.
You'll become a brain in a brain in a brain.

Greg Keeler teaches English at Montana State University and writes poetry and sings and paints and stuff, but because, after years of what his shrink calls self-medication, his mind is too addled to be much good at these things, he has taken to wandering up and down the rivers around Bozeman. This wandering would be aimless if it weren't for trout and mushrooms.

William Hjorstberg

ROAST CHICKEN STUFFED with FRESH HERBS and GARLIC

This recipe is an amalgamation of two classic French bistro dishes. The first, Chicken with Forty Cloves of Garlic, was told to me by Larry Edwards, the chef who created the original menu for the revitalized Chico Hot Springs dining room in the 1970s (his fabulous crisp bread sticks still grace every table there) and who currently owns the Grand Hotel restaurant in Big Timber. The second, I pieced together through trial and error, after enjoying many fine bistro meals and attempting to replicate those mysterious, succulent delights at home. The eighteenth- and early nineteenth-century French gastronome, Anthelme Brillat-Savarin once wrote, "Poultry is for the cook what canvas is for the painter."

Just as no masterpiece was ever painted on blotting paper, the perfect poulet roti depends upon the quality of the bird going into the oven. Thus, I strongly urge buying an organic chicken or free-range Hutterite fowl. Make sure to select one with untorn breast skin. Organic garlic would also be a plus, but peeling 40 to 60 cloves is quite a chore (although blanching them first for a minute or so in boiling water greatly lessens the ordeal), so I suggest the pre-peeled garlic available at Costco. Any fresh herb will do. Because of rosemary's pungency and the minute size of thyme leaves, if using these herbs instead of basil, I recommend half the amount.

1 whole roasting **chicken** *(3 to 4 pounds)*, at room temperature

40 to 60 large peeled **garlic** cloves *(or as needed)*

1 cup fresh **basil** leaves *(or $\frac{1}{2}$ cup rosemary or thyme)*

1 stick unsalted **butter**, at room temperature

1 teaspoon coarse **sea salt**

$\frac{1}{4}$ teaspoon freshly ground **black pepper**

$\frac{1}{2}$ cup **vermouth**

$\frac{1}{2}$ cup **water**

Serves 4 to 5.

1. Remove the packaged liver, neck, and gizzard from the chicken's cavity (save for stock) and trim excess fat. Rinse the bird, inside and out, under cold running water. Dry with paper towels and set aside.

2. Combine 5 gloves of garlic, herbs, butter, salt, and pepper in a food processor and blend until smooth. Chill in the refrigerator until slightly firm (15 to 20 minutes).

3. Preheat the oven to 450°, making sure the rack is in the center.

4. Gently work your fingers under the chicken skin, starting at the rear cavity, and loosen the skin from the breasts and thighs, taking care not to tear it. Reserve 2 tablespoons of the butter/herb mixture and stuff the rest under the skin, distributing it evenly by pressing gently from the outside.

5. Stuff the chicken's cavity with all the large peeled garlic cloves it will hold (30 to 55), pin the cavity closed, and rub the remaining 2 tablespoons of the butter/herb mixture over the top and sides of the bird. Place the chicken on a folding rack in a roasting pan and add the vermouth and water to the bottom of the pan.

6. Place the chicken in the oven and roast for 20 minutes. Reduce the oven temperature to 350° and continue roasting until done (20 minutes per pound). Baste every 10 minutes with pan juices. If the liquid evaporates, add more vermouth or water. The chicken is done when the skin turns a rich mahogany brown and the juices run clear from a thigh pierced with the tip of a knife.

7. Allow the chicken to rest for 10 minutes before carving. Meanwhile, scoop the garlic from the cavity. If done, each clove should be creamy and soft as butter. If the garlic is under-cooked, bring the liquid in the roasting pan to a boil on the stove top and simmer cloves until done. Serve the chicken with the cooked garlic, such accompaniments as suit your pleasure, and a nice bottle of dry red wine.

From *Symbiography*, published by Sumac Press in 1973.

Buick covered the distance to the stairs in five long strides, nearly slipping on the wet flagstones before he reached the shelter of the balustrade. He started down, one step at a time, his back pressed against the rough ashlar masonry of the terrace wall. At the bottom, out of sight of the house, was a hidden pavilion and under the blue and gold awnings, a spitted calf turned, glazed and dripping, over a bed of coals. Of all the wonders seen today, the splendor of food in such profusion was by far the most magical and bewitching. The Nomad wandered spellbound in front of a long cloth-covered table, trying to associate trout jellied in aspic, terrine of pheasant, grilled spring lamb, fruit heaped on silver platters with his own memories of eating roots and porridge, when a bit of dog or an occasional rat trapped among the grainsacks was a prize addition to the stewpot.

The rain whispered on the taut canopy of the pavilion; the coals hissed and snapped. Buick waited, barely moving. There wasn't much time. The banquet table was prepared, the guests must not be far behind. Although his every instinct told him to hurry, Buick approached the feast with the dignity of an invited God. A hind-quarter from the broiled calf stood on a thick wooden salver. The Nomad leaned his musket against the table and cut a slice with a surgically-keen knife. He had never tasted anything so good. He would take as much meat as he could carry. The knife, too. It was a beautiful knife; no one in the clan owned such a knife. He leaned forward and cut another slice. Good, good, the voice behind him said. Eat.

William Hjorstberg is the author of eight books of fiction, including *Alp, Gray Matters, Nevermore*, and *Falling Angel* (filmed as *Angel Heart*). As a screenwriter, he is best known for *Legend*, directed by Ridley Scott. Winner of a Wallace Stegner Creative Writing Fellowship and two Playboy Editorial Awards, he lives near McLeod on the Boulder River and is presently completing a biography of Richard Brautigan.

HUNTER and GATHERER CHICKEN

¾ cup **chicken stock** or broth that you have stalked in the grocery store

1 ounce **dried morels** that you have gathered at the farmer's market

½ pound fresh cultivated **mushrooms,** procured at aforementioned grocery store

4 tablespoons sweet **butter**

¼ cup **shallots,** finely chopped

Salt and freshly ground **black pepper,** to taste

⅓ cup **port wine**

⅓ cup **heavy cream**

3 **boneless chicken breasts,** skinned and halved

Parsley, chopped

Serves 5 in Manhattan,
3 in Montana.

1. Boil chicken stock. Put it in a bowl with dried morels and let stand for 2 hours.

2. Clean and slice store-bought mushrooms.

3. Melt butter in a skillet. Add shallots and sauté gently for 5 minutes.

4. Add chicken and brown on each side. Set aside.

5. Drain and chop morels. Add morels and store-bought mushrooms to the skillet, season with salt and pepper, and sauté on medium heat, stirring occasionally, for 10 minutes.

6. Preheat oven to 350°.

7. Add reserved soaking liquid, the Port, and the heavy cream to mushrooms and simmer for another 5 minutes, or until sauce is thickened.

8. Spoon mushroom mixture into shallow baking dish. Arrange chicken breast halves on top of the mushrooms. Season with salt and pepper to taste and cover baking dish with foil.

9. Set dish on middle rack of oven and bake for 20 to 30 minutes, until chicken breasts are done. Sprinkle with chopped parsley.

10. Serve over wild rice. Or the tame version.

From "*Etiquette*," published in *Salamander* in 1994.

The skillet rang as I slammed it on the stove and started to cook the onions. Maurice was in the hospital dying. My boyfriend Sam hadn't called. I was 23, unmarried, and back in Bridger, Montana, my hometown, living with my great aunt. The onions sputtered as I shook salt over the pan.

"As I was saying," Auntie May shouted to me from the next room. "Maurice was crazy about me, writing me letter after letter from Nicaragua, sending telegrams. And telegrams were expensive in those days. And on Valentine's day once, when we were courting—isn't that today, Eleanor?—he rode horseback to the Theta house and stopped under my window and sang."

"How wonderful," I shouted back. I opened the mushroom soup and dumped it, wiggling, in the pan.

"And when the housemother came to chase him off," she continued. "He apologized, handed her a bunch of hothouse roses to be sent up to me, then he turned around and galloped down Arthur Street."

"What a character," I said, turning the heat up on the burner, hoping the sizzling would drone out the sound of her voice. My boyfriend was in Alaska, doing God knows what—he sure as hell wasn't calling me—and I didn't want to hear about flowers or songs under windows.

As I carried the salad into the dining room, she looked up at me from a ladder-backed chair. "And you know what he sang?"

"How about dinner?" I said, smiling for all I was worth.

"'Let Me Call You Sweetheart,'" Auntie May warbled, swaying back and forth in time to the music.

"Aren't you hungry?"

"'Let me call you sweetheart, you belong to me.'"

"Don't you want to come to the table?" And don't you want to stop singing? I thought as I laid out silverware and napkins and the crystal goblets that tinkled and sang what sounded like love songs.

She stopped and watched me from one of the ladder-backed chairs that lined the dining room. "Water glasses on the right," she said.

"The right," I moved the glasses. "Of course."

"Oh, there I go again, getting in your way," She put her hand over her mouth. "I'm sorry, Eleanor. It's just that you need to know these things, dear—how to give a dinner party, how to set a table correctly, where to put the name cards and the salad forks and the wine glasses—they just don't teach these things."

Caroline Patterson is an editor at Farcountry Press in Helena, Montana. She has published fiction and nonfiction in *Big Sky Journal*, *Epoch, Newsday, Seventeen, Southwest Review*, and *Sunset*. A 1990-2002 Stegner fellow and recipient of the 1992 Jackson Prize in Fiction, she received a 1999 fellowship from the Montana Arts Council. She is working on a novel, as well as cooking with her husband, Fred, and her children, Phoebe and Tobin.

ALBERT GARCIA'S CHICKEN TORTILLA CASSEROLE

Albert Garcia worked with me as a nondegree candidate in the MFA program at the University of Montana during the mid-nineties. When he left Missoula, he left as his legacy his first book of poems, Rainshadow, *published in 1996 by Copper Beach Press, and this immortal Chicken Tortilla Casserole, a monument to the true writer's desire to spend as little time as possible in the kitchen and still produce one of the most delicious casseroles ever. Albert's most recent book is* Skunk Talk, *and he is now Dean of the Language and Literature Division at Sacramento City College.*

1 large **chicken**

6 **corn tortillas**

1 can **cream of mushroom soup**

1 can **cream of chicken soup**

1 small can diced **Ortega chilies**

$\frac{1}{2}$ pound **cheddar cheese**

$\frac{1}{2}$ pound **jack cheese**

Serves 5.

1. Cook chicken in water, drain, and bone.

2. Place corn tortillas, torn in pieces, in the bottom of a 9-inch by 13-inch pan. Place chicken on tortillas.

3. Mix cream of mushroom soup, cream of chicken soup, and diced Ortega chilies in a bowl and pour over the chicken.

4. Grate cheddar cheese and jack cheese. Sprinkle over top.

5. Bake at 350° for 45 minutes or until bubbly.

From "Old Hands" in *When the Earth Begins to End*, published by Copper Canyon Press in 2000 and used by permission.

…"So many years I've loved the way you buttered
my toast, spread my strawberry jam….

Now, though we live on smoke
mostly, in the faint plume of banked
cookfires underneath my

thin blankets,
whether it's your hands
or mine fumbling

at the doorknob, it's your voice
in my root cellar always.
Sweet as canned plums

and other fruits, flashes
of fabulous jackpots
light up like furnaces, roast

Patricia Goedicke is the author of 12 books of poetry, the most recent of which, *As Earth Begins to End*, was recognized by the American Library Association as one of the top 10 poetry books of the year. Other books include *Invisible Horses, Paul Bunyan's Bearskin*, and *The Tongues We Speak*, which was named a *New York Times* book of the year. All three were published by Milkweed Editions in 1996, 1992, and 1989, respectively. Currently she teaches one graduate poetry workshop a year in the creative writing program of the University of Montana, where she has been a member of the poetry faculty since 1981. She is the recipient of many awards for her poetry, among them a Rockefeller Residency at its Villa Serbelloni in Bellagio. Recent and forthcoming work may be seen in *The Boston Review, The Yale Review, The Denver Quarterly, Gettysburg Review*, and *Volt.*

TURKEY-VEGETABLE LOAF

The great thing about this recipe is that it's quick, provides protein in my generally meat-less diet (fish and poultry only) and saves time by holding one entrée in reserve. A great timesaver!

1 to 2 tablespoons **margarine**
(*1 if you use cooking spray*)

1 small **onion,** peeled and finely chopped

1 clove **garlic,** peeled and diced

1 small **carrot,** peeled and coarsely grated

2 pounds **ground turkey**

½ cup fresh **bread crumbs**

2 **egg whites**

¾ teaspoon **salt**

1 teaspoon ground **cumin**

½ teaspoon ground **cinnamon**

½ teaspoon **turmeric**

⅛ teaspoon **cayenne pepper**

Makes 2 8-inch by 4-inch loaves, 4 servings each.

1. Spray loaf pans with cooking spray or coat with 1 tablespoon of the margarine

2. Sauté onion and garlic in the other tablespoon of margarine in small skillet until soft (about 5 minutes). Cool slightly and combine in large bowl with all other ingredients.

3. Pack the mixture into the prepared pans. Cover one with plastic, then with foil, and freeze. Bake the second in a preheated 350° oven for 50 minutes. Drain off excess liquid. Cool 10 minutes before slicing.

From a poem titled "Three Things That Make Me Outrageously Happy in March" in *Spectral Waves*, forthcoming from Copper Canyon Press in fall 2006 and used by permission.

When navel oranges,
kissed by lazy California sun, glow like
moons in every supermarket, I go
crazy, buy all I can carry. At home, they
tumble from the sack to kiss my eager lips, and as
that nectar of the gods floods my veins, I live
in lovers' paradise every juicy moment
of Seattle rains.

Madeline DeFrees is an Oregon native who, for 38 years, was a member of the Sisters of the Holy Names of Jesus and Mary, where she was known as Sister Mary Gilbert. She was dispensed from her religious vows in 1973. DeFrees taught in the University of Montana MFA program from 1967 to 1979, when she moved to Amherst to teach in the University of Massachusetts MFA program for 6 years. Her honors include an NEA grant and a Guggenheim poetry fellowship. Her book, *Blue Dusk: New & Selected Poems, 1951-2001*, won a 2002 Lenore Marshall Prize and a Washington State Book Award. Seattle Pacific University gave her the First Annual Denise Levertov Award. Her eighth collection, *Spectral Waves*, is forthcoming from Copper Canyon Press in 2006.

BIG HOLE LAMB ROAST or
WHY THE WOLVES LEAVE YELLOWSTONE

Beg, borrow, buy, steal, or marry your neighbor's lamb, grass fed at 6,000 feet in the Big Hole Valley. Have it wrapped and frozen in Dillon or, if you're not hungry, take it to Big Hole Taxidermy: "You snuff 'em, we stuff 'em."

3-to 4-pound **lamb roast**

Olive oil

Garlic

Salt and **pepper**

Rosemary

Herbes de provence *(available from a specialty food store)*

1. With lamb this good, you don't do too much. Thaw roast (if frozen) the day before and remove from fridge 5 to 6 hours before cooking.

2. Drench with excellent olive oil, stick in some garlic, and pat on salt, pepper, extra rosemary, and herbes de provence. Let sit at least 2 hours at room temperature.

3. Prepare a shallow pan that fits in your gas grill, and enough aluminum foil to wrap the meat.

4. Preheat your grill to high. Braise the meat over open flames, with the grill top closed, for 2 to 4 minutes until it's brown or even black, turning as needed. Turn grill to low, to let it cool a bit.

5. Wrap the meat in foil and place in pan (no rack needed for lean natural lamb). Cook for 10 minutes on low, then cook on medium for another 20 minutes. Heat varies from grill to grill, but the roast should be bubbling without the juice boiling away and smoking. Begin checking at 30 to 40 minutes total cooking time; grills cook much faster than ovens. Meat thermometers are nice—if you have one, use it.

6. When the meat is very rare, turn off the grill and let the roast sit, grill top still closed, for 5 to 10 minutes, to warm throughout. The cuts should be medium well at the edges, rare in the middle. Serve with any juice left.

From *Borneo Log: The Struggle for Sarawak's Forests*, published by University of Washington Press in 1995, winner of a 1995 Western States Book Award.

Bill Bevis is retired from the University of Montana, where he taught American and Montana literature for more than 20 years, and lives in Missoula. He has written books on Wallace Stevens's poetry, on Montana writers, on the logging in Borneo, and a novel on a Death Valley prospector, Shorty Harris. He was on the editorial board of *The Last Best Place*.

After the party—yesterday—Jewin's pet myna bird awakened us at dawn. We ate our breakfast of rice and gathered for good-byes. Jewin's father was headman before him; a beautiful, diminutive old man with traditional tattoos and stretched ears, he had, without a word of English, been with us throughout our visit. As tribal elder, he had led off the dancing, and he and I had spent hours sitting on the edge of the hut platform plunking gourds with his blowpipe, children excitedly retrieving the darts. Among other presents, we had brought him a large map of the world, and when we left, he hugged each one of us, pointing very slowly and repeatedly in each of the four directions. Then he made a gathering motion into his stomach and spoke while Jewin translated, "Go, go far, in every direction, and then come back, come back." He seemed, without maps, to be telling us about the world—that it is very large, and small.

We hiked out though the forest, back to the clearing at Long Bangan.

Now, this morning, a few relatives are rising to send Richard and us downstream to Marudi. His aunt has built a fire in the "kitchen," a covered porch extending out from the back side of the longhouse. Her extended family, like most, has built its own kitchen adjacent to its living quarters in the longhouse. The cooking fire is laid on the floor in a contained bed of ashes a foot thick; pots and supplies are slung from wires above. A jar of water, a few shelves with utensils. Most of the smoke, which neither stings nor smells, goes out easily through the slat walls and eaves; the rest keeps mosquitoes away. We sit on the floor to a breakfast of weak coffee heavily sugared, white rice on a banana leaf, adark meat chunks that come from "some kind of cat," and sago; a gelatinous gray mass of pure starch pounded from the trunk of the sago palm. "The food is not what you're used to," Richard says, smiling. No one else around us understands English, and we all laugh.

5-to 7-pound fresh **pork shoulder**
(or a fresh ham)

For paste/marinade:

$\frac{1}{2}$ to $\frac{3}{4}$ cup trimmed **pork fat** (if the
shoulder is lean, use extra olive oil)

$\frac{1}{4}$ cup **olive oil** or more to thin puree

2 teaspoons **kosher** or **sea salt**

$\frac{1}{2}$ cup **Italian parsley**

10 fresh **sage leaves**

1 teaspoon **fresh rosemary**

2 teaspoons fresh or 1 teaspoon
dried **thyme**

1 **bay leaf**

1 teaspoon **coriander seeds**

1 teaspoon **pepper flakes**

1 teaspoon **pepper**

8 cloves of peeled **garlic** (1 head)

For sauce:

1 to 2 cups **stock**

$\frac{1}{2}$ cup ripe **tomatoes,** chopped

4 tablespoons **orange juice**

Half a **lemon**

Pinch **sugar**

Serves 6.

PORK ROAST with GARLIC and HERB CRUST

This is a recipe for slow-roasted, fall-apart pork. It looks difficult but it's very forgiving: You can vary the herbs in the paste—mint is delicious, or you could have a Mexican-style roast and use fresh coriander and chili powder—and you can use wine instead of orange juice for the sauce. The important thing is to give the pork at least a day to marinate in the paste.

1. If you have a shoulder with skin, peel it off and save for roasting, score the fatty side into diamonds, and rub it with salt and olive oil. Trim any excessively fatty portions of the roast, but try to keep at least a $\frac{1}{4}$-inch.

2. Puree the paste ingredients in a food processor or blender and rub over the pork roast.

3. Cover and refrigerate, ideally overnight.

4. Preheat oven to 325°. Place the roast in a heavy pan. If you have the skin, place it fat side down on top. Roast for 2 hours, then pour off some of the (considerable) fat. If you have the skin, put it fat side down underneath the roast. If the roast seems to brown too early, turn the oven down to 300°. Continue roasting another 2 hours or until the meat is soft and the fat crisp.

5. Drain the skin on paper towels, cut into strips and sprinkle with salt. It isn't healthy, but it's delicious.

6. Drain off most of the fat and deglaze the pan with the sauce ingredients. Carve the roast and serve the sauce on the side with potatoes or egg noodles and a salad.

From *Blue Deer Thaw*, published by Hyperion in 2000.

And in complete rebellion against financial reality she insisted that the wedding would be served, and haute: a caviar toast, followed by a seated procession of courses that, at the very least, would include a bisque, preferably lobster, and something involving foie gras and truffles. And even though she wouldn't be having more than a sip, each course would be served with an appropriate fine wine.

This was the problem. Peter wanted the food and wine they ate and enjoyed on a daily basis, which wasn't to say he wanted pigs in blankets or Cold Duck. He'd suggested a buffet with plenty of appetizers and three loose main course choices: a daube of some sort, roast quail, pork loin, or a baron of beef; and sides of salmon, either poached or grilled, with several sauces.

The eighty-dollar-a-head differential on these two visions was only part of the problem, though no one involved was rich. The quarrel over the menu was so vicious and childish that Jules decided Peter and Alice had boiled down every small wrong they'd inflicted or endured since they met, and now the mess had foamed out of control.

Jamie Harrison lives in Livingston, Montana, with her husband and two children and is the author of six novels, including *Blue Deer Thaw*, *The Edge of the Crazies*, *An Unfortunate Prairie Occurrence*, and *Going Local*.

Ossa:

3 pounds assorted **pork chops**

2 medium **onions**

3 cloves **garlic**

2 tablespoons dried **basil**

1 tablespoon **coriander seeds**

2 teaspoons **salt**

1 teaspoon **fennel seeds**

$\frac{1}{2}$ teaspoon each **nutmeg** and **red pepper flakes**

1 29-ounce can **Roma tomatoes**

2 cups jug or box **wine**, any color

2 **bell peppers,** 1 red and 1 green

1 6-ounce can **tomato paste**

Grated zest of half a **lemon**

1 bunch of **parsley,** chopped

Stracci:

3 large **eggs**

1$\frac{3}{4}$ cups **semolina**

$\frac{1}{2}$ cup **flour**

1 teaspoon **salt**

Serves 8.

BONES and RAGS (Ossa e Stracci)

Butte was a melting pot from its first boom days, but the Italian suburb of Meaderville, loved by locals and praised internationally, won out as THE place to go dining. Its style has even survived its being swallowed up by the Berkeley Pit in the 1960s, thus all Butte folks, regardless of ethnic upbringing, love to eat and to cook Italian. This is an original recipe evoking many traditional Italian flavors, but it is severely frowned on by my old Meaderville high school buddy, who alleges that real Italians would never use pork for anything other than sausage and salami.

○○○

Ossa:

1. Trim chops of fat, cut into thumb-sized pieces, 1 inch by 2 inches, and leave that much meat on each bone piece as well.

2. Chop onions coarsely into finger-joint-sized pieces ($\frac{1}{2}$ inch by 1 inch).

3. Mince garlic cloves.

4. Combine all in a large covered pot with spices, juice from tomatoes, and wine. Cook briefly on high to boil off alcohol, then cover and simmer for 50 minutes.

5. Chop red pepper and tomatoes like onions and green pepper half that size. Add to pot and simmer another 15 minutes.

6. Stir in tomato paste and lemon zest and simmer another 5 minutes.

Stracci:

1. Combine eggs, flours, and salt, adding water, if needed, 1 tablespoon at a time to make a dry dough.

2. Knead briefly to integrate, divide into 3 balls, let stand covered for up to several hours.

3. After adding peppers and tomatoes to sauce, roll out each ball using a pasta machine, starting with several passes at setting #1 to knead, then a pass each at #3 and #5, flouring in between to prevent sticking.

4. Tear or rough-cut each of these thin lengths into "rags" about 1 inch by 4 inches.

5. After adding tomato paste to sauce, cook pasta in rapidly boiling water until al dente, about 3 minutes. Drain and coat lightly with olive oil to hold.

6. On each plate, dish sauce partially alongside pasta, not smothering it, and sprinkle all with chopped parsley. Serve with fine-grated Romano cheese. Accompany with tossed salad, sesame bread sticks, and wine of choice (you could pull a cork now). Provide a bone plate. If fresh pasta is too time consuming, the sauce is great with any commercial pasta or with polenta. *MANGIA!* & *SLAINTE!*

(Note on cheese: if only it were widely available, it would be wonderful to substitute grated Cacciacavallo cheese for the Romano. Who else but the Italians would have the aplomb to name a cheese after horseshit! It's a great match for "Bones and Rags," and in its string-wrapped little balls, it's a perfect ivory replica of the "road apples" that dot backroads Montana.)

Jim Driscoll writes an arts column for the *Montana Standard* and was a Governor's Appointee to the Montana Committee for the Humanities. He is a retired high school English and science teacher and has directed drama and writing programs in Spokane, New York City, Lynbrook, and Butte.

111

Jim Driscoll

Written in memory of my mother, Eva Rummel Driscoll, b. Helena, 1898; d. Butte, 1976; a vivid and evocative storyteller and a deft and creative self-taught seamstress, who could never accept that the term "artist" could apply to such as herself.

For Eve

There's no heat in the gas!
Gram says
There's no taste to this dang fruit!

The apples from trees shading her Helena valley home
Bit sweet and crisp, shared with her porcelain doll
Now Seven-Elevens and Quik Stops sell soggy snacks
Where cows grazed by the Prickly Pear

The sun shone warm as she waded in pleasant ponds
Formed after the gold dredge ripped up the good land by her farm
Now tract houses have tidied up the miners' mess
But left a crammed flatness unkind to kids or ducks

But any day now
Gram's going to toss off that afghan and
Slip into something in pongee
Or maybe crepe de chine
Moss green, with her own hand beading

She'll crank up her Leaping Lena
Cram a few more Sheiks and Shebas into the rumble seat
And raise a dust cloud clear out to Broadwater and beyond!

The music will be hot and the water hotter
All the old gang will be there
Their pains melting away
In the steam of that great glistening pool
Even the dope-fiend will come out of the shadows, clean and smiling
And the apples will be the sweetest anyone's tasted
Since Adam

MOROS y CHRISTIANOS

Since I am lazy to the point of being sloth-like, I am fond of this easy recipe, useful when more friends than you wish you had descend and require feeding. Moros y Christianos *is a black bean, pork, and rice mix that is the national dish of Cuba.*

○○○

1. Dice onion, brown in a useful slop of olive oil.

2. Brown pork sirloin cubes, season with chili-garlic sauce. Add black beans.

3. Cook 2 dry cups of rice to instructions.

Your guests may find their own proportions of rice and meat and beans. This rewards individual initiative and they have only themselves to blame. Tart poppyseed coleslaw and good beer go well with this.

If you need your solitude back, simply add dangerous amounts of chili-garlic sauce or if hard-pressed, habañero sauce. Listen for gasps and look for the half-frozen expressions of the ambushed. Them as has weapons and don't use 'em . . .

For my recipe for Terribly Hazardous Chili, supplicants must send a one-hundred dollar bill and a self-addressed stamped envelope to P.O. Box 666; Livingston, Montana, 59047.

1 large **onion**

Olive oil

1 **pork sirloin roast,** cut into $\frac{1}{2}$-inch cubes

Sriracha *(or any chili-garlic sauce)*

1 can **black beans,** rinsed

2 cups **rice,** cooked

Serves 4.

Peter Bowen's newest addition to his mystery series is *The Tumbler: A Montana Mystery Featuring Gabriel Du Pre.* His previous books include *Badlands, Long Son, Yellowstone Kelly: Gentleman & Scout, Wolf, No Wolf, Coyote Wind,* and other mysteries.

Frances Kuffel

$\frac{1}{2}$ pound small **white beans**
(*pea or navy*)

4 cloves **garlic,** peeled and crushed,
plus 1 tablespoon minced garlic

1 medium-large **onion,** chopped

2 **carrots,** peeled and cut into chunks

2 cups cored and chopped **tomatoes,**
with their juice (*canned are fine*)

3 or 4 sprigs **fresh thyme** or
$\frac{1}{2}$ teaspoon dried thyme

2 **bay leaves**

$\frac{1}{4}$ pound slab **bacon** or **salt pork,**
in 1 piece

4 sweet **Italian sausages,**
about $\frac{3}{8}$ pound

1 pound boneless **pork shoulder,**
chopped in 1-inch chunks

2 **duck legs** (*Yeah, that'll happen. Go
ahead and use chicken. Or capon.
Capon is always good.*)

Chicken, beef, or **vegetable stock,**
or water, or a mixture, as needed

Salt and freshly ground **pepper** to
taste

1 cup plain **bread crumbs,** optional

fresh **parsley,** chopped for garnish

Serves 4.

SLOW-COOKER CASSOULET

When Passing for Thin *was reviewed in the* New York Times, *it was called cassoulet "in the French manner prepared by Julia Child..." I was so excited that I called my friend Noelle and asked her to dinner, then headed to Key Food to make the only celebration dinner that fit the day.*

1. Combine beans, crushed garlic, onions, carrots, tomatoes, thyme, bay leaves, and meats in slow cooker (or crock pot as eBay would have it) and turn heat to high. (If you like, brown sausage and bird legs in skillet before adding.) Add stock or water to cover by 2 inches. Cover and cook until beans and meats are tender, about 5 hours on high heat, 7 hours or more on low.

2. When done, add salt and pepper to taste, along with minced garlic. If you like, remove cassoulet from slow cooker and place in a deep casserole; cover with bread crumbs and roast at 400° until bread crumbs brown, about 15 minutes. Garnish and serve.

From *Passing for Thin: Losing Half My Weight and Finding My Self*, published by Broadway Books in 2004.

Food transmuted from pleasure to fantasy, and I had a very active imagination. I ate when I was lonely or bored, not an infrequent condition after my mother found her sweet Lucy in the post-Vatican II kumbaya glory days of the Church. I could make all the promises of the children's canon come true. Food was a flying carpet, Mr. Peabody's Wayback Machine, A Wrinkle in Time, the magic wardrobe, The Secret Garden.

Books, movies, and musicals were real to me and are forever stamped with the foods they featured. The bare necessities for the Prince Christopher Rupert Windamere Vladimir Karl Alexander Reginald

Lancelot Herman Gregory James's ball that included six hundred suckling pigs and marshmallows ("for roasting") were just about right. Food was "My Own Little Corner" and Leslie Ann Warren's Cinderella was my kindred spirit in daydreaming. And oh! the heaps of corn and lobster in Carousel were a fine thing to visit Maine in search of.

I pondered the gustatory exotica of my books. How could I make maple syrup harden as Laura and Mary had in the Big Woods? What were the "sweetmeats" that popped up in "Aladdin and the Wonderful Lamp"? I read "Hansel and Gretel" with the shame of a double agent. I would have eaten the bread rather than mark my path through the woods with it, and I'd have sold my soul to have my way with the gingerbread house. So, too, I doubted I would offer to carry the Christmas muffins to the Hummels as that brat, Amy, did in her one-upmanship over my heroine, Jo, in Little Women. I lusted for and tried to approximate it all:

Heidi's toasted cheese and bread (where could I find goat's milk?); the smell of hot buttered toast that "simply talked to Toad" in The Wind in the Willows; the chocolate cake bobbing against the ceiling in Mary Poppins; Eliza Doolittle's chocolates in a room somewhere; apple strudel, schnitzel, and noodles from The Sound of Music.

Julie Andrews may be personally responsible for a good ten pounds of the weight I magically amassed.

It gives new meaning to devouring books.

Frances Kuffel is a native of Missoula, Montana, and received bachelors degrees in religious studies and English from the University of Montana. An MFA from Cornell University deluded her into thinking a PhD from New York University would be nice; consequently, she has worked in publishing for 17 years as a literary agent. She's published short fiction and poetry in *The Georgia Review, Tri-Quarterly, Prairie Schooner, Glimmer Train,* and *The Massachusetts Review.* Her memoir, *Passing for Thin: Losing Half My Weight and Finding My Self* was published by Broadway Books in 2004. She lives in Brooklyn and is currently working on a second nonfiction book.

BAKED HAM LOAF

As a kid this was my favorite meal and I thought of it as absolutely exotic—nearly out of reach for a normal Wyoming family. My mother reinforced that belief by only preparing her ham loaf once a year, as a gift to me on my birthday.

○○○

1. Mix together meat, eggs, milk, bread crumbs, and pepper. Shape into a loaf.

2. Stir the sauce ingredients in a roasting pan, then place the loaf in the sauce and bake in a 350° oven for 2 hours. Turn loaf after it has baked 1 hour.

○○○

The loaf:

2 pounds **ground ham**

1 pound **ground pork**

2 beaten **eggs**

1 cup **milk**

1 cup **bread crumbs**

Sprinkle of **pepper**

The sauce:

$\frac{1}{2}$ cup **brown sugar**

1 tablespoon **mustard**

$\frac{1}{4}$ cup **vinegar**

$\frac{1}{2}$ cup **water**

From the essay "Wapiti School" in *Where Rivers Change Direction*, published by University of Utah Press in 1999 and reissued by Riverhead Trade Publishers in 2000.

The school had no cafeteria. We all packed lunches. They were brought in brown paper sacks or black, steel lunch pails. I don't remember much plastic wrap. There was a lot of waxed paper and tin foil, which most of us were required to scrape clean, refold and return to our mothers. Most of those same mothers had been teenagers during the Depression and weren't about to have their children precipitate another.

I've always believed a packed lunch to be an accurate barometer of a child's family. Sort through a lunch pail and know a family. Are the parents creative or dull? Practical or innovative? Lazy, poor, uncaring? Most of our mothers cared. Most of them considered bologna part of a balanced diet, but most of them viewed bologna a luxury. Standard fare was an apple, a sandwich, perhaps a candy bar. I've seen sweet potato sandwiches. Once, in the early fall a mayonnaise and sliced zucchini sandwich. A lot of elk, deer, mountain sheep, and moose sandwiches. Twice a turnip sandwich. Nothing went uneaten.

It was from those Wapiti lunches that I gained an almost religious confidence for the free market system. What was one boy's garbage was another's manna. My brother's and my fall and late spring lunches were packed by a cook who worked our lodge dining room. He was an exhausted and alcoholic old bachelor, and provided two specific seasons of fried egg sandwiches. The bread was homemade but the eggs were never drained and their yokes consistently sunny side up. When we peeled back the waxed paper what we found was a gray and yellow fist-sized wad of dough, congealed bacon grease and yoke. We saw a mess. The Krone boys saw an entree. Their eyes would widen when we held our lumps of sandwich to the sun. Their nostrils flared. Not every day. But the majority of days. I have no explanation for it. Their father was the district Forest Ranger, a decent man with decent tastes, and their mother a cheerful woman, and one of the best cooks in the valley. Perhaps they ate too well? Or perhaps Pete and Kip's fondness for fried egg sandwiches was a simple example of grace? We didn't care. My brother and I traded the things for cookies, brownies and squares of fudge. Everybody went away a fuller, happier boy.

Mark Spragg is the author of *Where Rivers Change Direction*, a memoir that won the Mountains and Plains Booksellers Award, and the novels *The Fruit of Stone* and *An Unfinished Life*. All three books were top-ten Book Sense selections and have been translated into 13 languages. He lives in Cody, Wyoming.

Neil McMahon

Meat:

One chunk, red. (*This scenario is geared to a beef roast of about 3 pounds. If larger or smaller, adjust proportions and cooking time. There's no need to buy expensive cuts—actually, not doing so is kind of the point. I've had the best luck with things like sirloin tip and eye of round. Rump and chuck are also good—rump tends to be a little chewy, and chuck, on the greasy side. I haven't tried it with game, but I'd think that elk, venison, or buffalo would work fine.*)

Vegies:

One large **yellow onion,** cut in good-sized chunks, not minced.

Several **carrots,** peeled and chopped to finger size.

A few Idaho **potatoes,** peeled and quartered lengthwise.

Spices:

One packet of **onion soup.**

Salt, a bunch of it.

Pepper's good.

If you want to get fancy, **garlic** in any form.

1 or 2 tablespoons of **parsley,** and anything else that blows up your lederhosen.

Wine:

Optional. If you use it, use red, dry, and cheap.

LONELY BOY POT ROAST

It's been said that revenge is a dish best eaten cold. This pot roast is a dish best eaten by single guys living in squalid digs and scratching out a living at some menial job while harboring loftier aspirations. (Although women and even children, if sufficiently hungry, have been known to partake.)

The two best things about this recipe are that it's really easy and it doesn't use the word "roux."

Ingredients: On top of those listed below, more imaginative chefs than myself, which includes pretty much everybody this side of the rodent kingdom, will benefit from additions and variations.

○ ○

1. Preheat oven to 325°.

2. In medium roasting pan, add about 4 cups water and wine in any ratio you like (I usually go 3:1 water to wine; more wine makes richer sauce).

3. Stir in onion soup packet (a quick stir is fine—it will dissolve with heat). Add salt and other spices as desired.

4. Put roast in pan. Douse with broth. Sprinkle more salt directly on meat, along with anything else you want to soak in, such as pepper and garlic.

5. Cut up onion and add to broth.

6. Cover pan and put in oven.

7. Go back to your loser life.

This next step isn't necessary, but I take out the roast after about 3 hours, turn it over, cut off any obtrusive fat, re-baste, and re-spice. With salt, for example. Put back in oven for another hour or so (4 hours total cooking time). If you're going to leave it there longer, turn heat down to 200°, and at 5 hours, turn temperature to warm.

When to add other veggies depends on timing. Potatoes take an hour or so at full temperature. Carrots are quicker—call it 30 to 40 minutes. Both need longer if heat is down. Spuds stand up well to long immersion, unless you like them crisp. Carrots get soggy, so watch it if you're fussy.

Other remarks:

One of the beauties of this is that you can start the roast at lunchtime and let it go on into the evening if you turn down the heat, as mentioned above—the meat will be fine. Reheats great. Perfect for sandwiches all week. Remnants also make dandy beef Stroganoff, Mexican food, and other such gourmet dishes that you can create with a small investment in a spice packet from your friendly neighborhood grocery store.

From *Twice Dying*, published by HarperCollins in 2000.

Monks went to the refrigerator and took out the evening's centerpiece, a thick filet mignon. The cats closed in like sharks, using his absence that day as leverage for tyranny. He distributed succulent bits of raw steak until the swirl of fur around his ankles turned to the more pressing business of paw-washing and naps, then put what was left on the hibachi.

He ate standing up in front of the wood stove: the filet charred just right, al dente linguine tossed with garlic and Parmesan, half an avocado soaked in vinegary blue-cheese dressing. He imagined he could feel his blood pouring to his stomach to aid digestion, leaving his body like a deflated balloon. By the time he finished washing the dishes, he was in a half-dream. He walked down the hall to his bedroom. He put the photos back in his safe, but left the Beretta on his dresser, and fell into bed.

Neil McMahon was born in Chicago in 1949. After attending Stanford, he moved to Montana in 1971. Since then, he has spent most of his life either working as a carpenter or writing. He has published four novels with HarperCollins. His short fiction has appeared in *The Atlantic Monthly*, *The Best of Montana's Short Fiction*, and others. He's married to Kim Anderson (the compiler of this cookbook, which raises the issue of who you have to sleep with to get published around here). They live in Missoula.

SMORNA PA ZOSA (untranslatable)

My mom learned this recipe from my dad's mom who came straight from the old country in steerage to Stockett. Icve talked to any number of other Slovenes and even Croats and no one had ever heard of this concoction, though I suspect I've just not spoken to the right tribe. Smorna pa Zosa is primarily dinner, though it's wonderful the next day and has the rib-sticking quality you might need if you were headed out to shovel a few tons of coal. In our family it is much revered, and there is much slavering and spoon-licking and the raising of eyebrows as the whole thing comes together. (This is not required in its preparation.)

This recipe will feed about 8 to 10 Slovenes, 12 normal humans, and possibly 15 polite WASPs. There were 6 kids in our family, 9 in my dad's, but the recipe is seemingly unreduceable. Advanced math skills might allow you to figure how to make this for 2 or 4 but no records remain of this having been made for anything less than 10 or so. Too, the name seems to be untranslatable, or at least I've not found any such words in my Slovene-English dictionary (yes, such a thing does exist). Among the Tri-City (Stockett, Centerville, Sand Coulee) Zupans it just means something like "Heaven on a Plate."

Note: For the second-generation kids, my mom tamed things down, but Grandma Zupan used enough cayenne pepper in the original to bring tears to your eyes. So season to taste. Janet and I will revert to the old-country ways when the kids are all gone. We'll have to invite company.

Zosa:

4 pounds **top round,** cubed

1 small **onion,** diced

$\frac{1}{4}$ cup **flour**

2 cups **water**

1 to 2 teaspoons **paprika**

$\frac{1}{2}$ cup **ketchup**

1 teaspoon **cayenne pepper**

Salt, to taste

Smorna:

18 **eggs**

3 cups **milk**

3 cups **flour**

$\frac{1}{4}$ cup **sugar**

1 teaspoon **salt**

Oil

Serves 10 to 12.

Zosa:

1. Over high heat, sauté cubed meat in oil until it begins to brown. Add onion and continue cooking until onion is translucent and liquid has cooked almost completely down.

2. Add flour (enough to coat meat). Brown the flour.

3. Add up to 2 cups water and continue cooking at high heat for 2 more minutes.

4. Turn heat to medium-low. Work with a spoon to scrape the sides and bottom of the pan clean.

5. Add paprika, ketchup, cayenne pepper, and salt to taste.

6. Stir to blend, taste, and add more of the seasonings, as desired.

7. Simmer for 1 hour, add more water, as needed, and recheck for seasonings.

Smorna:

1. Beat eggs until fluffy.

2. Add milk.

3. Add up to 3 cups flour slowly—mixture should have the consistency of a gravy.

4. As mixture thickens, stir in sugar and salt.

5. Coat a skillet liberally with oil and set on stove turned on medium-high heat.

6. Slowly coat the pan with $1\frac{1}{2}$ cups batter. Allow mixture to cook a bit, then mash it to the consistency of scrambled eggs. Prepare the Smorna in small batches; keep cooked portions warm in a 250° oven.

7. Serve *Smorna* smothered in *Zosa*. Enjoy!

Kim Zupan grew up on the east side of the Rockies in Stockett and Great Falls. He worked for several ranches in the Judith Basin and spent a decade as a professional bareback rider with the Professional Rodeo Cowboys Association, besides working as a commercial fisherman and a carpenter. He received his MFA in fiction from the University of Montana in 1984. His stories have appeared in *Epoch, Big Sky Journal, Hunting's Best Short Stories, The Best of Montana's Short Fiction, The New Montana Story,* and others. He is married to Janet Schmidt Zupan. They live with their children in Missoula.

From *The Carrion-Eaters,* unpublished.

Jimmy shed his coat and collapsed on the bed for a profound theatrical sigh. He shucked his crutches from his forearm and unfastened a leg.

"Goddamn, that's some good smelling roadkill. What're we having?"

"Hun." Hickney donned an oven mitt and slid the tray from the oven. Four tiny partridge wrapped in bacon crackled in a puddle of grease.

Jimmy said, "God, I think I like hun better than anything."

With a spoon Hickney basted each breast carefully and tugged a miniature leg bone. "I believe they're ready for your holiness."

Hickney set out two huge potatoes split from baking and spooned onto their plates boiled cabbage from a steaming pot. They set upon the birds like famished Vikings, conversing with grunts and raised eyebrows and greasy smiles over the tops of beer bottles. Jimmy stropped his empty plate with potato skin as Hickney watched.

"I can't have you eating the plate. I only have the two."

ZACHARY WINESTINE'S MARINADE for STEAK or LONDON BROIL

This recipe, which has become a staple at our house, was the brainchild of Zachary Winestine, a director of photography and filmmaker (States of Control [1998] and Caravan/Prague [2004]) who divides his time between Greenwich Village and a cabin on Montana's Rocky Mountain Front.

Zack stands in a truly distinctive Montana cultural tradition. His grandmother, Belle Fligelman Winestine, daughter of Helena pioneer merchant Herman Fligelman, was chief assistant to Montana's Jeannette Rankin in 1916 when Rankin became the first woman elected to the United States Congress. While in Washington, D.C., Belle met Norman Winestine, and the two soon married. In the early 1920s, the young couple expatriated to Paris, where Norman served as correspondent to The Nation. *The Winestines then returned to Helena, where Norman took charge of the Fligelman family business. Belle was a writer in her own right, publishing short stories in* The Atlantic *and other national journals. Norman served as chair of the Montana Historical Society board for many years, and both Winestines contributed mightily to Montana cultural life.*

Belle and her sister Frieda Fligelman—poet, polymath, and founder of the discipline of sociolinguistics—will be featured in Harriet Rochlin's forthcoming A Mixed Chorus: Jewish Women in the American West, 1849–1924.

1. Cuts of top sirloin or London broil, preferably deer, elk, bison, or grass-fed Montana beef.

2. Mix ingredients together and marinate meat for 2 hours or more. Then grill or broil.

3 tablespoons **olive oil**

3 tablespoons **lemon juice**

2 large cloves **garlic**

$\frac{1}{2}$ teaspoon **jalapeño flakes**

Dash of **red pepper flakes**
(or cayenne)

Generous twist of **black pepper**

$\frac{1}{2}$ teaspoon dried **basil** or **oregano**

1 **bay leaf**

From *The Suburb of Long Suffering*, published by Bedrock Press in 2002 and used by permission.

Breakfast Poems

> for Elizabeth A.

BLOOD ORANGES SPIT
>   across the front page
of the *Times*, and you sip
>   black coffee.
Nothing new, just the comfort
>   of the foreseen,
the joyful usual. Bless
>   this morning, my
friend. Sip black coffee.

THE CATS FACE OFF,
>   their tails swollen,
their claws safely hidden.
>   You cheer them on,
your face sleep-furrowed,
>   your beautiful eyes
drowsing. The cats leap
>   out of harm's way.
You bless their stratagems,
>   their fearless trepidation.

Poet, editor, and independent scholar **Rick Newby** is the author or editor of 15 books. Most recently, he edited *The New Montana Story* (2003) and *The Rocky Mountain Region*, in the *Greenwood Encyclopedia of American Regional Cultures*, selected by *Library Journal* as one of the best reference series of 2004. He also served as coeditor of *Writing Montana: Literature under the Big Sky* (1996) and *An Ornery Bunch: Tales and Anecdotes Collected by the W.P.A. Montana Writers' Project* (1999). Newby's latest collection of poems is *The Suburb of Long Suffering* (2002).

A native of Kalispell, Montana, and a member of the Montana Center for the Book's statewide advisory committee, Newby now makes his home in Helena, where he serves as executive director of Drumlummon Institute.

Ralph Beer

1 large **white onion**

1 16-ounce can **Dinty Moore beef stew** (check expiration date).

Salt, to taste

Serves more than enough.

Ralph Beer has worked as a ranch hand, swamper, clerk, cannon cocker, logger, heavy equipment operator, battery rat, carpenter, and whiskey taster. He and his wife, Maggie, recently sold the Howard Beer Ranch and have gone on to other things, though they dearly miss their cows. Beer is the author of the Spur Award–winning novel *The Blind Corral*, and the essay collection *In These Hills* has been reissued recently by The University of Nebraska Press. His essays have been included in the anthologies *The Last Best Place* and *Montana Spaces*.

RAGOUT CELIBATAIRE

Prep time: 33 seconds.

Cooking time: a couple minutes on Grandma's woodstove

1. Preheat woodstove to cherry red (use lots of pinch pine roots and kerosene to get her going fast).

2. Peel away outer layers of onion.

3. Dump stew into medium-sized saucepan, place on stove, and stir rapidly until lightly carbonized.

4. Put saucepan on old newspapers on table. Crack open latest Neil McMahon novel. Splash a couple spoonfuls of salt on stew. Read. Eat. Best served with several half-frozen Coors Tallboys. Eddy's white bread is a great accompaniment to this dish.

5. While gnashing down stew, take occasional bites of onion to dull flavor.

6. Continue until exhausted.

7. Throw remainder outside for tomcat and magpies.

SWEDISH MEATBALLS

This is how I made Swedish Meatballs every year at Christmas time and still do. I learned it 60 years ago in Sweden.

○○

1. Combine hamburger, cornflakes, eggs, and spices.

2. Put butter or margarine in frying pan and fill pan with meatballs.

3. Slide frying pan back and forth over the hot plate, until meatballs are browned on all sides.

3 pounds **hamburger**, rolled in big 1$\frac{1}{2}$-inch meatballs

3 cups **cornflakes**

4 **eggs**

Spices to taste: **salt, pepper, curry powder, dill weed, parsley, allspice**

Butter or **margarine**

Hanneke Ippisch was born and raised in the Netherlands. She became a resistance worker during World War II, when her country was invaded by Germany. She was imprisoned and released in April 1945, and then she worked for Queen Wilhelmina of Holland. She moved to the United States in 1956 and is the author of *Sky: A True Story of Courage During World War II*, *Spotted Bear: A Rocky Mountain Folktale*, and *Small Moments*. She lives on Flathead Lake.

125

Jeanne Dixon

2 pounds **hamburger**

Salt and **pepper**

1 cup of **flour** (more or less)

Blue cheese or **Roquefort**

¼ pound **butter** (not margarine)

Wine

Cooked **rice** (not instant)

JOHN WORTHINGTON MEATBALLS

I got this recipe from a young man I was in love with many years ago. This is simple and quick, yet hearty enough for a winter night and can be quite elegant.

1. In large mixing bowl combine hamburger with salt and pepper, form into 3-inch balls.

2. Roll each ball in flour. Make indentation in each ball and stuff with blue cheese.

3. Using a large skillet, brown the stuffed meatballs in butter. When they are pleasantly browned, put a lid on the skillet and allow them to cook slowly until thoroughly done.

4. Add wine to the meatballs, a little at a time, to make a sauce of the desired thickness.

5. Pour meatballs and wine sauce over a bed of hot rice and finish off the bottle of wine. Serve with hard rolls and a crisp green salad. For dessert, try warm poached pears with a trim of chocolate syrup.

From *Fish-Mom*, unpublished.

At her request, summer Sundays were reserved for fishing. "Your dad's dad was shot down by lightning for working on the Lord's Day," she said, and she didn't want that sort of thing to happen to us.

So like it or not, my two younger brothers and I set aside any hopes or plans we might have entertained and helped Mom load the long black Hudson, its trunk thrown up and doors flung open like the wings of a long black beetle, engine thrumming, while Dad got the fish poles down from the hay barn, angling them across the back seat so that the ends poked out a back window with strips of red cloth to flutter from each, in case of violation.

The Hudson, with its plush (if somewhat blood-spattered) interior, had once been a Death Car for big city hoodlums. After my dad got hold of it in one of his mysterious horse-trading deals, it would serve out its days as a stately sedan for two highly contentious adults, three squabbling kids, an excitable moustached ten-pound terrier, and a loud-mouthed Siamese cat on harness and leash who fought to ride up front on Mom's lap no matter how many times she tossed him in back. Then find a place for Dad's big metal tackle box (filled with fishline, silver spinners, bobbers, reels, assorted hooks and flies, a Prince Albert tobacco can packed with struggling angle worms, and a can of whole kernel corn, and a bag of last year's marshmallows to use as bait in case nothing else worked); plus room for the banged-up galvanized washtub we used as a picnic hamper. Looking back, it could only have been the miraculous stuff she packed into this tub that prevented us from killing each other… bowls of perfect fried chicken: young roosters taken as they basked unafraid in the sunshiny garden, killed before they knew they'd been caught, cut up and rolled in seasoned flour, fried in hot fat in black iron skillets (lid off until browned, lid on and the heat turned to Medium-Low and

cooked until done—no pink at the bone!—lid off and sizzled on High for that crisp brown skin we really shouldn't eat, but do). So delicious!

And her First Prize Potato Salad, kept on ice until scooped onto mismatched plates. Never runny, never dry: hard-boiled eggs and potato chunks mixed with mayonnaise and a tablespoon of yellow mustard, add finely diced dill pickle and plenty of little green onions hurried in from the garden, chopped and folded in (green tops and all), salt to taste, with a dash of paprika across the top for color. She'd be up all night baking: her best yeast rolls to eat with churned butter and raspberry jam; Devil's Food Lightning Bolt Layer Cake (secret ingredient: a can of drained sauerkraut added to the batter at just the last minute) with Double Fudge Frosting half an inch thick. Such richness. Such wealth. All those long years of childhood, how could we have thought we were poor?

Jeanne Dixon is a fourth-generation Montanan, born on Two Medicine Creek on the east slope of the Rockies where her father was a trapper and then manager of a large sheep ranch. The family later farmed in the Flathead Valley. Jeanne got an elementary teaching certificate and taught at schools in various sections of the United States, from the backwoods of rural Kentucky to migrant camps in California's Central Valley. Later she spent time in Russia, Scandinavia, and Great Britain. Her short stories have been published in literary magazines and anthologized in *Montana's Best Short Fiction*, *The Best of Northern Lights*, and *Pushcart Prize Stories*. She has written seven young adult novels. Presently, she lives in Missoula with a speckled cat named Mango and is working on a novel about family life in rural Montana.

MIRIAM BALLS

Miriam Goodall was the nurse on duty in the Helena hospital where I was born. Her mother-in-law, a Montana pioneer, taught school up Last Chance Gulch, and her father-in-law was an assayer. My folks were hard rock miners. Her recipe for meatballs is a family favorite. Chilled leftovers can be sliced and served in a sandwich.

Meatballs:
1 pound **ground beef**

$\frac{1}{4}$ pound **ground pork shoulder**
(or pork sausage for more spice)

1 **onion,** finely minced

$\frac{1}{2}$ cup raw **rice**

1 beaten **egg**

1 cup fine **bread** or **cracker crumbs**
(or seasoned bread crumbs for more spice)

1 cup hot **milk**

Salt and **pepper,** to taste

Dash of **allspice**

Sauce:
1 can **cream of mushroom soup**

1 cup **water**

$\frac{1}{8}$ teaspoon **pepper**

$\frac{1}{4}$ teaspoon **salt**

$\frac{1}{2}$ tablespoon **Worcestershire sauce**

Meatballs:
1. In a large bowl, mix together meatball ingredients.

2. Shape into meatballs about the size of a golf ball and arrange gently in 2 layers in a 2-quart casserole.

Sauce:
1. In a small bowl, mix together sauce ingredients.

2. Pour sauce over meatballs, covering them completely.

3. Bake covered at 350° for $1\frac{1}{4}$ hours.

4. To thicken sauce, cook uncovered for last 10 to 15 minutes.

Lyndel Meikle, ranger, historian, and blacksmith at Grant-Kohrs Ranch National Historic Site in Deer Lodge, is the author of *Back at the Ranch*, which has run in Montana newspapers since 1982. She located and edited the memoirs of John F. Grant (complied as *Very Close to Trouble*), which was published by Washington State University Press in 1996. She has written several chapters in the popular *Speaking Ill of the Dead: Jerks in Montana History* and its sequel, *Still Speaking Ill of the Dead.* She collects quotes, a favorite being, "You know, an alligator's got four legs, and he cain't go up more'n one creek at a time."

BIGOS

Magda the ravishing translator who sweetens

the university's dull dun-colored hallways and

especially my office is offering to teach me

about *bigos* (beegos), a classic Polish dish, yes?

So, three kinds of meat, two kinds of cabbage,

plus apples, onions and prunes, plus of course

garlic and wine. And don't forget dried mushrooms!

Which we must never fail to moisten at night, okay?

Also, she warns, everyone in Warsaw is an expert on this

and further, no one can trust another completely

to get the recipe right—it's a question of Slavic

blood and so forth—but, raising a sculpted eyebrow,

we have no serious quarrel about watching the pot.

As with a man and a woman, she whispers, haste

and a distracted mind bring only disaster. I notice,

I say, how the lips in producing the Polish for cabbage,

kapusta (kapoosta), hers as well as mine, spring forward

on the middle syllable as if approaching something

deliciously hot. We are having an experience, do I

wish to study *bigos*-making or not, she says, for

to begin with we must pursue, now, a good fresh start, yes?

Then we select from a barrel our sauerkraut and God

knows how many tiresome socialist lines (Poland is under

Communist rule at the moment, not that it matters

much to the dish), rolling lush green eyes,

Gary Gildner lives in Idaho's Clearwater Mountains, a nice bike ride from Missoula. His 20 published books include *Blue Like the Heavens: New & Selected Poems; Somewhere Geese are Flying: New and Selected Stories;* the novel *The Second Bridge;* memoirs *The Warsaw Sparks* and *My Grandfather's Book;* and *The Bunker in the Parsley Fields,* which received the 1996 Iowa Poetry Prize. He has also received a National Magazine Award for Fiction, Pushcart Prizes in fiction and nonfiction, The Robert Frost Fellowship, the William Carlos Williams and Theodore Roethke poetry prizes, and two National Endowment of the Arts Fellowships. Gildner has been writer-in-residence at Reed College, Davidson College, Seattle University, and Michigan State University and has been a Senior Fulbright lecturer to Poland and Czechoslovakia.

to stand in for ham, beef, and kielbasa, though her

personal view is the onions go nicer with duck.

Well, I say, we must have duck then and why not

venison too for its long, lean leaps over the ample

fields of barley and oats, its ruddy antlers

glazed by the spring moon and those steamy snorts

as it pulls up short to circle three, four, five

cocky times around the scented and receptive doe?

My grandmother, Magda says, a great beauty with

an enormous appetite, always insisted the more game

the tastier, but my mother, whom many say I favor,

though I am not positive about that, believes one wild

meat is sufficient. Normally. And you, Magda?

Oh, I believe *bigos* should have personality—

And like my grandmother, who survived three very robust

husbands and was considering a fourth, perhaps

the handsomest of all, but unfortunately he fell

from a horse, I believe *bigos* should never be eaten

until a week of reheatings has happened

and of course by this time you are quite, quite eager.

Visitation Night, Dinner for Two

Our King Salmon date, we call it, habanero
No matter what's on our plates, pasta, watermelon, the black olives
She mounts on her fingertips, to sing,
"I choose you…and you…"
But this night it's true: a fresh

Fillet I've baked with lemon and lots
Of garlic—to keep witches and fibbers
With slitty eyes and nasty colds off our backs.
We like to flow smooth, to wiggle our tails
Among rainbows, till everything comes up true
As the fairy slippers we sometimes find
On our walks in the woods (when lucky's a thing
We can even behold). "As I was saying, my dear,
Have you found any bones?" she inquires.
She is six. "Three as a matter of fact." "Oh, delightful, let's share—
I found only one."
We finish with chocolate ice cream, double dips,
Then I wash, she wipes, drying each fork and spoon
As if it's a prize for next time.
        During our story upstairs
(which we reach thanks to our great silvery strides)
she holds her stuffed dog Blackie, my hand,
the plastic Baggie containing her two thin bones
and the one wish she's made twice—yes, of course
I know why: Once that dunce, sometimes forgets it!
After the poor boy Lucky captures the Golden Feather
From the terrible griffin and can keep the king's
Beautiful daughter, my little swimmer
Is soon drifting off, happy that goodness wins out.
I give her two kisses, yes just to make sure.

Pat and Carol Williams

The crust:

3 cups **flour**

½ teaspoon **salt**

1 cup **shortening**

½ cup cold **water**

The filling:

2 large **potatoes,** diced

2 cups **onion,** diced

½ cup **parsley,** chopped

Salt and **pepper**

1 pound **beef steak,** diced

2 tablespoons **butter**

Serves 4.

Pat Williams served as a U.S. representative for Montana from 1979 to 1997. He is now a Senior Fellow and regional policy associate at the Center for the Rocky Mountain West and serves on several advisory boards. He is a regular columnist for several newspapers in the Northern Rockies and teaches at the University of Montana. His coffee table book, *Montana*, features an essay by him and photographs by Salvatore Vasapolli.

IRISH PASTIES

I was raised in Butte, Montana. My parents were in the restaurant and candy business—with restaurants, lunch counters, and homemade candy outlets throughout the city.

I remember with deep fondness the city's vibrancy in my earliest year—the late 1930s and early '40s. On many weekend nights, our largest restaurant, with the unique name of The American Candy Shop, would remain open until two or three o'clock in the morning.

For decades Butte teemed with people intent on good food, fun, entertainment, hard work, and good paydays. That unforgettable city helped spawn Montana and encourage our economy, and it lies indelible in our memories.

1. Sift flour and salt together. Cut in shortening. Add water, mixing well.

2. Divide dough into quarters. Roll out each section so that it is thin, round, and the size of a pie pan.

3. For filling, combine potato, onion, and parsley.

4. Pile quarter of mixture on one side of each rolled pastry, keeping it within an inch from the edge. Add quarter of beef to each pile. Season with salt and pepper and dot with butter. Fold empty half of pastry over filling, crimping edges together and slitting top of each.

5. Place 2 pastries on a pie pan. Bake at 400° for 30 minutes. Reduce heat to 350° and bake 30 minutes more. May be frozen and stored.

VENISON/ELK

If I am preparing elk or venison for someone who's never had game before or who's had a previous bad experience with game, this is the recipe I turn to. It's also a recipe I cook for myself at least once a week.

○ ○

1. In a mixing bowl coat steaks with mustard.

2. Heat olive oil in cast-iron skillet or frying pan until it shimmers, on the verge of smoking. Add crushed garlic and salt and pepper to hot oil. Sear steaks in oil on first side for as long as it takes to raise blood on the uncooked surface.

3. Turn, add red wine, and cook for half as long as first side. If, for example, the first side takes 2 minutes to raise blood on uncooked surface, cook second side for 1 minute. Serve with hand-cut French fried potatoes and Caesar salad.

○ ○

3½ tablespoons **Dijon mustard**

6 to 8 tablespoons **extra virgin olive oil**

1 clove **garlic,** crushed

¼ teaspoon **salt**

¼ teaspoon **black pepper**

1 tablespoon **red wine**

Serves 4.

An avid outdoorsman, **Mark T. Sullivan** is the author of 6 novels and has been published in 14 languages. He lives in Bozeman.

From *The Purification Ceremony* published by William Morrow & Company in 1997.

My parents followed a personally crafted religion based on the old ways passed down from their Micmac and Penobscot ancestors, as well as ceremonies and prayers the woods and the rivers suggested to them. Distilled to its essence, the moral underpinning of their days was one of living in accord with the laws of nature: take only what you need when you need, adhere to the seasons and their fruits, try to live as simply as possible, as if you were a primitive hunter, gatherer....The hunting of birds and deer, casting for trout, the gathering of nuts and berries, and the daily preparations in the kitchen were the rituals they celebrated.

VENISON-HUCKLEBERRY STEW
(in memory of Jim Welch)

I don't really recall where I learned of this stew, or if it is something I assembled from various sources. I like to think of it as a Native American stew. The Indians of the Northern Plains and Rockies often mixed berries with their meats and their pemmican to add flavor and nutrients. Like the Woodland Indians serving cranberries on turkey, this was another way of ingesting that essential, life-giving, scurvy-preventing substance that Western scientists now call vitamin C.

European cuisine also sometimes mixes fruit and meat, because the acid of the fruit provides a natural meat tenderizer and tanginess.

I improvised the following recipe for the occasion of James Welch's memorial potluck, in August 2003. I thought the choice appropriate because Jim, of course, was a Montana writer and a member of the Blackfeet Tribe. The guests quickly wiped the pot clean. Now, whenever I make this stew, I think of Jim.

2 pounds or so **venison round** or **roast**

2 quarts **huckleberries** *(can be frozen and thawed)*

3 small **onions** *(Hmong-grown onions, if possible)*, diced

Several cloves of **garlic,** minced

2 tablespoons **oil**

Splash of **thyme-flavored vinegar**

1 to 2 teaspoons **sugar** or **honey**

Salt and **pepper,** to taste

1. Mash huckleberries in a bowl until runny.

2. Slice venison in thin strips.

3. Marinate meat in bowl of mashed huckleberries in refrigerator for several hours.

4. Sauté onion and garlic in oil in large, deep frying pan or wide pot.

5. Add huckleberries and meat mixture.

6. Add a few splashes of thyme-flavored vinegar and sugar, salt, and pepper to taste.

7. Simmer gently 3 hours or so until meat begins to fall apart and huckleberry juice mixture is reduced to a thick sauce.

From *Driving to Greenland*, published by Burford Books in 1994.

We've met the hunters only a few days before, on a sunny afternoon in early July, when Amy and I had found Mamarut Kristiansen standing in his hunting whites eating a hamburger topped with shredded red cabbage at the counter of the Polar Grill. This resembles just another hot dog stand in, say, Ohio, providing you ignored the view out the front door of the five-story iceberg imbedded in the half-frozen sound. The Polar Grill sits on a rocky street in the middle of Qaanaaq, a town of about 100 houses that looks a bit like a Scandinavian fishing village dropped on a gravelly headland; there are a few bulk oil tanks, radio masts, dozens of kayaks, and hundreds of howling sled dogs.

That morning at four—clocks don't count here in the endless light of summer—Mamarut had dogsledded across the ice of Whale Sound into Qaanaaq with a load of mattak, the horn-like skin of the narwhal that is a Greelandic delicacy. With a handshake, Mamrut, a stocky, energetic,

fun-loving man in his early thirties and son of a famous walrus hunter named Masauna, agreed to take us out with him. Thus it was, a few days later, that we left his two-room house on Qeqertarssuaq (Herbert Island) and, with a kayaks lashed to the gunwales of his and Sigdluk's small motorboats, we headed across Whale Sound. We beached the boats, with a slow crunch of ice against fiberglass, on a great floe. "And now we can wait for hours and hours and hours," remarked our interpreter, Vito....

For dinner that first evening on the ice floe, Sigdluk fired up his campstove and boiled the party a pot of inaluaq—bearded-seal intestines. The snow crunched under our boots as we squatted around the pot and burned our fingers as we split open lengths of gut with our pocketknives. We stuffed them with wedges of seal blubber and gobbled them like hot dogs slathered with the works—fuel to stoke the body's furnace against the polar climate.

Peter Stark, a National Magazine Award nominee, is a contributor to *Outside*. His work has also appeared in the *Smithsonian* and *The New Yorker*. He is the author of *Last Breath* and *Driving to Greenland* and the editor of an anthology *Ring of Ice*. His newest book, *At the Mercy of the River*, was published by Ballantine Books in 2005. He is also the founder and partner in a small-diameter wood business, North Slope Sustainable Wood LLC. He lives in Missoula.

1 pound **steaks**, about 4 $\frac{1}{2}$-inch thick steaks

5 tablespoons **butter**

2 cloves **garlic,** minced

4 ounces **mushrooms,** sliced

$\frac{1}{4}$ cup **Marsala**

3 **green onions,** chopped

WHITETAIL STEAKS in MUSHROOM SAUCE

Letting the butter get a bit brown and richly caramel-like in aroma adds more flavor to the dish. But it's a quick moment: it begins to burn quickly. If you're nervous about it, just heat the butter to sizzling.

1. In a 9-inch skillet, melt 2 tablespoons of the butter over medium-high heat. When the butter starts to sizzle and smell rich and caramel-like, add the steaks. Cook for 3 minutes to a side for rare, 4 for medium. Remove the steaks from the pan and place on a heated platter in a warm oven.

2. Add the rest of the butter to the pan, and let it get richly caramel-smelling again, then lower the heat to medium and sauté the garlic and mushrooms for about 3 minutes, or until tender. Add the wine and green onions and return the steaks to the pan. Spoon the sauce over the steaks and continue cooking another 2 to 3 minutes, until the sauce is hot again. Serve immediately.

This recipe is from The Venison Cookbook, *by Eileen Clarke. All John's and Eileen's books are available at www.riflesandrecipes.com.*

From *The Queen of The Legal Tender Saloon*, by Eileen Clarke, published by Greycliff Publishing in 1997.

I used to imagine my grandpa sleeping on the ground inside a circle of cow ponies; he could get up and ride anyone of them, anytime, anywhere, and not have to obey the Parkchester policemen yelling at us to keep off the grass. I'd imagine that Grandpa came to our apartment and camped on the living room floor with me to watch "Fury" and "My Friend Flicka" Saturday mornings when my father was working thirty-six hours straight putting in a show at the Coliseum and hadn't come home yet.

While I invented memories, my father only believed in truth. First his mother had died. Then Grandpa died of cancer, leaving Dad and his three sisters to St. Mary's orphanage. Each time I asked to look at Grandpa's picture, my father would tell me about his first job, the only job he could get: lookout, he said, for a bunch of lousymickrumrunners. He believed that was all one word, all one dirty type of man.

He wouldn't look at Grandpa's cowboy postcard when he took it out of his dresser drawer for me. He'd turn his back and look out our third-floor window, waiting for me to be done, saying it was work that made life good, not wandering around gawking, spending your money on phony nonsense. His hands would roll through the change in his pockets like gears turning in a clock.

ooooooooooooooooooooooooooooooooooooooooooooooooo

From "The End of Andros" in *The Life of the Hunt*, by John Barsness, published by Wilderness Adventures in 1995

Why do postcards and paintings of the Caribbean always show leaning palms and the wreck of an old fishing boat smack against the green water, when there are far more dead airplanes and cars? Why doesn't anyone paint the fuselage of a Cessna crumpled in the scrub jungle along the beach?

There was, of course, an old wooden boat lying rib-open on the beach below the lodge, picturesquely rot-ting between two palms. Of course the fisherman took several color slides of this boat, but none of the dozen or so dead drug planes he saw. He took a walk along the beach one day after lunch, while Jim fly fished in the surf. Jim caught a jack perhaps nine inches long. The fisherman found lots of plastic jetsam, including an airplane seat complete with seatbelts.

The Meat of the Story

ooooooooooooooooooooooo

Eileen Clarke is the author of 7 game cookbooks, and a novel, *The Queen of The Legal Tender Saloon*. Between books, she's written for *Gray's Sporting Journal*, *Field & Stream*, and *Successful Hunter* and has been married to John Barsness for ages and ages.

John Barsness, who was born and raised and is still living in south-western Montana, started writing about the same time he started hunting. He's published 7 books, including *Montana Time: The Seasons of a Trout Fisherman* and *The Life of the Hunt*, and hundreds of articles in magazines such as *Field & Stream*, *National Geographic*, *Sports Illustrated*, and *Gray's Sporting Journal*, where he also served as editor.

VENISON BURRITOS

When I was a kid growing up in Michigan, one side of my extended family more or less lived on poached deer. My grandfather—a French-Canadian trapper, he would have been called Metis had he lived in Montana—thought the neck of a newly killed deer was the best part of the animal. I still live mostly off venison (legal game) and wanted to figure out something to do with the neck, which almost nobody eats anymore.

Venison neck or 1 pound of **venison,** any cut

Olive oil

1 to 2 **garlic** cloves

1 big **onion,** chopped

Up to 1 cup of **cumin,** enough to coat meat

4 to 5 dried **red chiles,** crushed

Salt and **pepper**

Beer

Grated **sharp cheddar cheese**

Large corn or flour **tortillas**

Canned **enchilada sauce**

1. Using a pan big enough to hold the whole neck, brown it in olive oil.

2. Add in and sauté more chopped garlic cloves than you think necessary and onion.

3. Reduce heat and dump in about a cup of cumin, enough to coat the meat, then add 4 or 5 or more dried red chiles, crushed, and salt and pepper to taste.

4. Pour beer over the whole business, enough to almost submerge the neck, and simmer very slowly, making sure to add water whenever it threatens to go dry.

5. After about 4 hours, give or take, (depending on the deer), the meat will have simmered off the neck bones. Use a fork to finish stripping meat from the neck bones. Discard bones.

6. Wrap a couple of spoonfuls of meat and grated, sharp cheddar cheese in big corn or flour tortillas.

7. Either fry them in a little oil, or line them up in a shallow baking pan and cover with canned enchilada sauce and more grated cheese. Warm through in a 200° oven and serve.

From *Against the Grain*, published by North Point Press in 2004.

The goal of attending to the nutrition of people is radical, but I don't think it radical enough. Food is about a great deal more than nutrition. It along with sex forms the pathway that connects our species to the future. Evolution hinges on survival, which in turn hinges on nutrition and reproduction. We have other needs, oxygen for instance, but these are automatically met. We must hunt for food and sex. This hunt is our obsession, our drive, the focus of our senses, our sensuality, so ingrained as to define our humanity. These drives are our essence.

Somewhere along the line we became so focused and so competent in this hunt that we rigged the outcome. To hunt is to be insecure about the immediate future, the nagging fear of want that has driven us to our worst excesses and finest creations. Agriculture rigged this game by allowing storage and wealth ensuring future food (and sex). Agriculture dehumanized us by satisfying the most dangerous of human impulses—the drive to ensure the security of the future. In this way we were tamed.

Yet the hunter and gatherer survives in each of us. When a woman ambles through the Union Square market and the deep purple glint of plum catches her eye, she replicates a primal process. She awakens pathways of primal signals. The process itself is satisfying, human. When she speaks with the farmer who grew it, she connects to a bit of her community, our link to the rest of humanity. We subvert agriculture every time we re-establish that link. Our weapon in this is sensuality.

Richard Manning is the author of 7 books: *Against the Grain*, North Point, February 2004; *Food's Frontier*, North Point, October 2000; *Inside Passage*, Island Press, November 2000; *One Round River: The Curse of Gold and the Fight for the Big Blackfoot*, Henry Holt, 1998; *Grassland: The History, Biology, Politics and Promise of the American Prairie*, Viking, 1995; *A Good House: Building a Life on the Land*, Grove, 1993; and *Last Stand: Logging, Journalism and the Case for Humility*, Peregrine-Smith, 1991.

Jim Harrison

3 pounds of lean hindquarter **black bear**

2 pounds of slaked **hominy,** nixtamal

2 tablespoons toasted **cumin**

2 tablespoons **Chimayo** or **hatch ground chile**

1 head **garlic**

Serves 6.

Jim Harrison is the author of four volumes of novellas, seven novels, seven collections of poetry, and a previous collection of nonfiction. The winner of a National Endowment for the Arts grant, a Guggenheim Fellowship, and the Spirit of the West Award from the Mountains & Plains Booksellers Association, his work has been published in 22 languages. He lives in Montana and Arizona.

BEAR POSOLE

I had this dish years ago in the Sierra Madre and have made it several times myself to avoid letting gift meat go to waste.

1. Cut bear meat into inch cubes.

2. Simmer with slaked hominy, nixtamal. Canned hominy is no good.

3. Add cumin, chile, garlic.

4. Simmer until meat is tender, usually 2 hours. Mexicans improve this dish with a cleaned calf's foot but pig's feet work to improve broth.

From *The Raw and the Cooked: Adventures of a Roving Gourmand*, published by Grove Press in 2001.

My search for the genuine in the food in my life came about slowly and certainly wasn't a product of how I grew up in the upper Midwest, a region notorious for its bad food. Perhaps the only thing that saved our senses was the two months a year our gardens were operable in this sour climate. My own obsession with food began in my late teens with reading and budget travel. In the Midwest the common diet draws most heavily from the worst aspects of the Scandinavian and the German, coupled with an attitude summed up as "we eat to live not live to eat" as if this were an assigned moral choice. Added to this is the historical move from the agrarian to the city, which comprises the demographic revolution of the twentieth century—a move from growing and gathering your own food to jumping in a car for the trip to the supermarket.

SHO'S ANTELOPE ROAST

I must credit my friend Seonaid Campbell with this recipe. I stood over her for most of New Year's Eve 2004, fearing that she'd overcook the meat from her first antelope. She did not overcook it. It was a yearling, so the roast from its hindquarter wasn't very big, enough for four people. This is not a recipe for the minimalist chef, or for the cook insisting on precision at all points. You'll have to intuit your way, believe when you feel you are failing. Drinking red wine during preparation is advisable. Try the same recipe with venison.

1. In a clay garlic roaster, roast 1 head of garlic sprinkled with olive oil until soft.

2. Marinate roast for an afternoon in olive oil and small amount of tarragon vinegar or port. After it has adequately marinated and a few hours before serving time, preheat the oven to 350°.

3. Quarter chop the shallots, leaving the skin on.

4. In a cast-iron pan (or skillet), put in enough butter and olive oil to lightly cover the bottom of pan, and heat on high. Sear one side of the roast. Flip the roast and remove the pan from the heat.

5. Place a small amount of fresh sage leaves and rosemary under the roast. With tooth- picks, pin strips of organic bacon to the top of roast. Place shallot quarters around the roast in the pan.

6. Place the pan in the oven and cook until the temperature of the meat in the center is 120°. Check the meat temperature with thermometer every 5 or 10 minutes. Be diligent about checking, because lean game will continue to cook long after it is removed from the oven.

7. In the meantime, squeeze the roasted garlic from its shell and set the garlic mush aside.

1 to 2 heads **garlic**

Antelope roast

Olive oil

Splash of **tarragon vinegar** *(optional)*

Port wine

6 big **shallots**

Butter

Handful of **fresh rosemary**

Handful of **fresh sage**

3 to 4 strips of **organic bacon**

Salt and **pepper**, to taste

½ cup of **heavy cream**

Stephen Byler

Stephen Raleigh Byler, whose grandparents were Amish, was born in a small town in the Pennsylvania Dutch country near Lancaster. He earned an MA in religion and literature from Yale University and an MFA in fiction from Columbia University. In addition to writing and editing for numerous small magazines, Byler has worked as a radio announcer, a bankruptcy counselor, and a fly-fishing guide. He divides his time between Lancaster, Pennsylvania, and Livingston, Montana.

8. When the meat temperature reaches 120° (it will be very rare, but this is the only way to eat this meat), take the roast out and set it on a meat board (one that will catch the blood). Save roasting juices.

9. Remove the shallots from the pan and set aside. Remove crispiest parts of the shallots' skin (skin adds good flavor to the sauce) and add to roasting pan. The pan should contain juice from the meat and bacon, small bits of shallots, and softened rosemary and sage.

10. Turn the burner on medium-high heat. Deglaze the pan with a generous amount of port wine.

11. Add some butter, roast garlic mush, and any juice from the meat board. Salt and pepper to taste.

12. Reduce the sauce and turn the heat to low. Let the sauce simmer.

13. Stir in about $\frac{1}{2}$ cup of heavy cream.

14. Place the roast in serving dish with shallots around and garnish with fresh rosemary and sage. Pour port wine/cream reduction sauce over roast and serve.

○ ○

From *Searching for Intruders*, published by William Morrow in 2002.

When the waiter leaves, she reaches across and pinches my cheek like a child.

"You're not very clever, are you?" she says.

I just stare at her.

"Who do you think will pay my bills when I'm gone?" she says.

"Your insurance?"

"I don't have insurance."

"Your estate?"

"I don't own anything."

"I give up," I say. "Who?"

"No one, silly. I'll be dead." She

reaches in her purse and produces three Visas, an American Express, and a MasterCard. She spreads them out in her fingers like a hand of cards.

"Great. I'll pick out the wine," I say.

For a first course she orders quail on toast. She talks me into the wild boar pate.

"I love game," she says. She spreads some of my pate on her quail and then she breaks off the tiny drumstick and nibbles on the meat. "You can taste the life in it," she says.

For an entrée, she orders buffalo in a wild mushroom sauce. She tries to order for me again, but I insist on making my own choice this time. I get the flounder, poached in lemon and chardonnay.

"I'm in the mood for something light, okay?"

"Of course you are," she says.

When the waiter brings the wine and pours it for me to taste, she reaches across and snatches up my glass. She sips and nods approvingly and invites him to join us for a toast. He pours each of ours and pours himself a modest glass.

"To my body," she says.

"To your body," the waiter says, raising his glass, smiling slightly and looking generally confused.

When we are through with our entrees, she orders for me again.

"I'll have a cappuccino and so will he," she says. "How would you like yours, dear?" she asks. She leans over and touches the side of my face. "I'd like mine wet this time, I think. Yes, cappuccino wet for me," she says, smirking.

"And for you, sir?" the waiter says.

"Whatever," I say, feeling slightly embarrassed by her obsession with the texture of drinks, among other things. The waiter smiles and shrugs at me.

"Dry, I guess," I say.

"And what about dessert for either of you?" he says.

"Do you have something with meat in it?" she asks.

WILDERNESS SWEET TOOTH COOKIES

From *Indian Creek Chronicles: A Winter in the Bitterroot Wilderness*, published by Lyons Press in 1993

○○

To get ready:

Read all the mountain man stories you can. Watch Robert Redford in Jeremiah Johnson. Watch it again. And again. In fanatical emulation, agree to spend the next seven months in a tent in the middle of some northern wilderness, in the winter, alone. It helps if you've never done this before. Also if you've never cooked before. Then, buy all your food for those seven months in one day. There'll be no refrigeration. Go heavy on cans and dry goods.

Get dropped off in the wilderness. Dig a hole to keep your food from freezing. Drop your food in the hole. Bury it. Eat rice and beans for the next few months.

Begin to realize how long it's been since you've eaten anything sweet. Anything at all. Try a spoonful of sugar, as in the song. Gag. Dig the Betty Crocker cookbook out from under your spare long johns. Find you've only got all the ingredients for Brown Sugar Drops.

To begin:

Stir up the ingredients. Brazenly add uncalled-for cinnamon. Stare for the first time at the tiny potbelly stove that is heating your tent. Wonder how to preheat it to 400°. Look around, making sure no one can see you standing with a bowl of cookie batter, wishing for an oven. Remember you haven't seen anyone for months.

Get serious. From the woodpile, shovel out the old grill you found before the snow buried everything. Cut it to fit inside the stove. Use a file, because, before you came in, you couldn't see any reason to bring a hack saw. Scratch your head, trying to remember why you thought you'd need a file. Remember cookie batter instead.

Open stove and beat on wood, damping open flame. Decide it's 400°. Spoon batter onto scrap tin sheet. Set on rack in stove. Close stove. Without timer, decide to go by smell. Step outside to enjoy another storm. Watch snow falling without wind, big flakes sifting down muffling the world. Tilt your head back and see from how high you can follow a single flake's descent. Again check that no one is looking. Stick out your tongue and try catching only that flake. Laugh. Remember cookies. Jump into tent. Swear. Leave front flap of tent open to let out smoke.

Fill tin with new drops of cookie dough. Wait for fire to die out completely. Start second batch. Stay inside this time. Sit. Wait. Walk to open flap and shiver. Look at stump to see how much snow has accumulated. Turn, with determination, back to stove. Sit in front of it. Flip through cookbook, wondering what you might try next. Guess you'll skip Coquilles St. Jacques.

At the very first hint of second batch of smoke, flip open stove and pull tin sheet out. Scrape blackened cookies onto table. Study them until cool enough to touch. Cut blackened bottoms off with a Buck knife. Repeat process on tops. Sides. Think, in road miles, how far it is to a dentist. Convert this to months. Eat brittle center morsel carefully, letting saliva soften the crunch. Decide not to do this twice.

Drop last of cookie dough onto sheet. Look at coals, which have gone to gray ash. Shiver. Close front flap of tent. Set cookies onto grill rack. Close stove. Put on coat and hold hands on stove sides for warmth.

Wait as long as you can, until you think cookies are cooling inside stove, rather than warming. Remove tin sheet. Touch dough. Discover that, while not quite browned, dough is warmer than when put into stove.

Scrape cookie off sheet. Lean back in your chair, put your feet on table. Drop warm dough in mouth. Chew. Smile. Widen smile. Begin to ponder what you'll substitute for scallops when cooking Coquilles St. Jacques.

Serves 1.

Pete Fromm's story about his winter job babysitting salmon eggs for the Idaho Fish and Game in *Indian Creek Chronicles: A Winter in the Bitterroot Wilderness,* was winner of the Pacific Northwest Booksellers Association's 1994 Book Award. Pete is a five-time winner of the PNBA Award and also is the author of *As Cool As I Am, How All This Started, Dry Rain,* and *Blood Knot.* He lives in Great Falls, Montana.

The dough:

4 cups **flour**

1 pound **butter**

6 **egg yolks**

1 cup **sour cream**

1 box **confectioners' sugar** to be
used for rolling, filling, dusting

Nut filling:

$1\frac{1}{2}$ pounds **walnuts,** finely ground

6 **egg whites**, whipped to peaks
Confectioners' sugar to taste

1 tablespoon **rum** or **vanilla**

Lemon zest and **juice** to taste

Apricot filling:

1 bag of **dried apricots**

Water

1 cup **sugar**

AUNT THERESA'S KEEFLIES

When someone asked a panel of writers how we learned discipline, one said car mechanics, another tango. An only child, I became the keeflie baker, rolling thousands of 3-inch circles as I listened to the tales of a dwindling circle of elders.

Morning:

1. Cut butter into flour, add egg yolks and sour cream. Work until dough is smooth.

2. Shape into four rolls, wrap in waxed paper, and chill 8 hours.

3. Select fillings and prepare.

Nut filling:

1. Mix walnuts and sugar.

2. Fold in egg whites, add rum and lemon.

Apricot filling:

1. Simmer bag of dried apricots with enough water to cover and one cup sugar until soft, then mash.

Evening:

1. Preheat oven to 350°.

2. Cut chilled pastry into $\frac{1}{4}$-inch slices, then quarter these and roll into balls. Refrigerate, working with only half a dozen balls at a time.

3. Dust pastry cloth or waxed paper with flour and confectioners' sugar, roll pastry paper-thin, place walnut or apricot filling on one side and roll up. Shape walnut-filled keeflies into cigars, apricot-filled keeflies into crescents.

4. Place on greased cookie sheet, and bake 10 minutes or until light brown. Cool. Sprinkle with confectioners' sugar and store in air-tight containers.

From *Except by Nature*, published by Graywolf Press in 1998.

Charles Olson's "I, Maximus/ a metal hot from boiling water" might have been the lyric sung on the backlot of the body shop where I grew up—paint fumes, grease pans, sparks flying—surrounded by Serbs, Germans, Hungarians returned from the Second World War, men who saw themselves, no matter how confusing, in direct lineage from the gods. Oh there were the fallen—Dale, for instance, who lived on a houseboat in the middle of a cornfield, drove an ancient Cadillac convertible and stole women's girdles from clotheslines—but mostly these were supermen. I studied their calendars of women with bombshell breasts and skirts always given to the wind, and when I could get my hands on them, I read their nude sunbathing magazines. These were men unlike those I would meet in college, love or marry, but I studied them as we ate at my grandmother's table, the sounds they made so different from mine.

I grew up on an acre between Dixie Highway and the Illinois Central tracks where trains raced hourly through fields of wild asparagus. In the dream space between two lines of speeding technology was a grape arbor; a fish pond; a house full of women sunk to their elbows in bread dough; fields of geese, goats, sugar pear trees; the graves of bloody cars and grass grown crystalline through cracked windshields. I baked with the aunts and fished silently with the uncles and felt at home on the periphery of both worlds surrounded by action and accompanying sound. My grandfather whittled, sanded, banged, and snored. My grandmother—on a tonic of garlic and wine—fried, kneaded, waltzed. Together each day they spoke raucous Platt und Hochdeutsch. I did not participate in their conversation, nor the bodymen's jokes, the spray painting, the bumping and welding, the straightening of steel, though those too are dialects I know.

And when I went off to college, I lied. I denied that I had won blue ribbons for butterscotch bars and tight little stitches in skirts, because that was female, and I denied I'd grown up in a body shop, because that was laughable, lower class and not female. So began a dance, of learning, then denying experience. Not exactly the way to build intelligence, though silence sharpens the senses, creates an oily, pungent memory.

All's Well That Ends Well

Sandra Alcosser founded and directs the MFA program in creative writing at San Diego State University each fall; she directed SDSU's International Writers Summer Program at National University of Ireland, Galway, from 2004 to 2005. She is poet-in-residence for Poets House in New York, The Wildlife Conservation Society, and Central Park Zoo, and the poetry editor for *Parabola Magazine* and The Wildlife Conservation Society's *State of the Wild*. Her most recent book, *Except by Nature*, was selected for the National Poetry Series and received the James Laughlin Award from the Academy of American Poets. She has received numerous other awards, including two National Endowment for the Arts fellowships. Her poems have appeared in *the New York Times*, the *New Yorker*, and *The Paris Review*. Alcosser lives in and travels from the Bitterroot Mountains of Montana. She has been chosen as Montana's first poet laureate.

147

Greg Gordon

1 cup (2 sticks) **butter**

2 **eggs**

2 cups **brown sugar**

$\frac{1}{2}$ cup **applesauce**

  A few drops of **vanilla**

$2\frac{1}{2}$ cups **whole wheat flour**

2 cups **whole oats**

1 teaspoon **salt**

1 teaspoon **baking powder**

$1\frac{1}{2}$ cup **chocolate chips**

1 cup **raisins**

$\frac{1}{2}$ cup **flax seeds**

$\frac{1}{2}$ cup **nuts,** chopped

  Makes 24 cookies.

GREG'S HEARTY WILDERNESS COOKIES

These heavy-duty, high-energy cookies are great for wilderness pack trips or just plain eatin'.

○○○

1. Blend ingredients: butter, eggs, brown sugar, applesauce, and a few drops of vanilla.

2. Then add the following: whole wheat flour, whole oats, salt, and baking powder

3. Mix well, then add: chocolate chips, raisins, flax seeds, and chopped nuts

4. Mix well and spoon batter onto cookies sheets. Bake at 350° for 12 minutes.

From *Landscape of Desire: Identity and Nature in Utah's Canyon Country*, published by Utah State University Press in 2003.

We break into groups of three to cook dinner. Each group's meal looks remarkably like the next—a steaming pot of starch. Our stoves have two settings—high and off. Further limiting creativity is the need to fill three people to bursting with one pot of food. Most dishes consist of three steps: 1. boil water; 2. add food; 3. eat. In two months on the trail, one can weary of dried beans and rice, mashed potatoes, and mac and cheese. The monotonous consistency of "camp slop" can be offset by the addition of a food repair kit consisting of lightweight luxuries such as curry power, dried green chilies and jalapeños, dried vegetables (carrots, tomatoes, green and red peppers), Parmesan cheese, garlic salt, pepper, Italian seasoning, and cinnamon. So with unabashed self-interest at stake (the students will be feeding me as well), I prepare lavish meals at the beginning of a course in the hopes they will follow suit. "One-pot wonders," I call them.

Tonight I am preparing a simple but elegant meal with discrete fanfare. I begin by sautéing fresh chopped garlic, onion, carrots, sun-dried tomatoes, and pine nuts in olive oil. The aroma pervades the camp and the other cook groups enviously glance my way. With a flourish, I add basil and oregano. When lightly browned, I scrape this into a plastic bowl and set it aside in full view of the rest of camp. Then I boil a pot of water and add multi-colored pasta spirals. While the pasta is cooking, I add some of the hot water to the bowl mixing in dried milk and pesto. After draining the pasta carefully into a sump hole dug for our waste water, I pour the pesto mixture over the pasta. I sprinkle Parmesan cheese and salt just before ladling out portions. I glance over at the faces of the mashed potato eaters as my cook group exudes ecstatic proclamations over the meal.

Greg Gordon received his MS in Environmental Studies from the University of Montana in 1992. Since that time, he has been teaching university field studies programs in natural history, conservation, and nature writing. He has written two books and numerous articles. His latest book, *Landscape of Desire: Identity and Nature in Utah's Canyon Country*, explores the relationship between wilderness and the psyche. He lives in a yurt near the Dearborn River in central Montana.

Nora Martin

1 cup **nuts,** chopped

$\frac{1}{2}$ cup **butter** (1 stick), melted

2 cups **graham cracker** or **cookie crumbs** *(any kind work, including shortbread, chocolate, or oatmeal)*

1 6-ounce bag of **chocolate** or **butterscotch chips**

$1\frac{1}{4}$ cup **shredded coconut** *(sweetened or unsweetened)*

1 14-ounce can of **sweetened condensed milk**

Makes 24 cookies.

GRANNY KRETCHLEY'S LAYERED COOKIE BARS

These easy cookies are great because you can vary them with whatever ingredients you have on hand.

○○

1. Preheat oven to 350°. Butter a 9-inch by 13-inch pan.

2. Chop nuts and set aside.

3. Make cookie crumbs by using a blender or placing cookies in a plastic bag and crushing with a rolling pin.

4. Melt butter in baking pan in oven. Press cookie crumbs evenly on top of the butter to make the crust. Sprinkle the nuts over the crust layer.

5. Spread the chips over the nuts. Then sprinkle on the coconut.

6. Drizzle the sweetened condensed milk all over the top.

7. Bake 25 to 28 minutes until coconut is golden brown. Cool and cut into squares.

BROWNIES

1. Melt butter and chocolate together over very low heat. Cool to lukewarm.

2. Stir in sugar, eggs, and vanilla.

3. Mix together flour, cocoa, and baking powder, then stir the dry mixture into the chocolate.

4. Add walnuts and chocolate pieces, or leave them out if you choose. Pour the brownies into a buttered 10-inch by 10-inch pan. Bake at 325° for approximately 35 minutes.

○○○

From *Breath in Every Room*, published by Story Line Press in 2001.

Play
Give the body heat and it will
adjust, feel a chill. Another piece
of chocolate please, more sun,
the last bite of scallops. Maybe
a walk, it says, in the coulee
where the hawk flies. And
more love, says the heart.
It chases its tail, can't figure
what it's after. Mornings,
when I sit to pray, the dog
puts her paws in my lap,
licks my knuckles. I don't
know why she comes to play
whenever I close my eyes.

1 cup **butter**

3 ounces **unsweetened chocolate**

3 ounces **bittersweet chocolate**

$1\frac{1}{2}$ cups **sugar**

5 **eggs**

$2\frac{1}{2}$ teaspoons **vanilla**

$1\frac{1}{2}$ cups **unbleached flour**

$\frac{1}{3}$ cup **unsweetened cocoa**

$\frac{1}{4}$ teaspoon **baking powder**

$\frac{1}{2}$ cup **walnuts,** chopped

$\frac{1}{2}$ cup **bittersweet chocolate pieces**

Makes 9 brownies.

Tami Haaland is the author of *Breath in Every Room*, which won the Nicholas Roerich Prize from Story Line Press. She teaches at Montana State University–Billings. She was raised on the Hi-Line, attended the University of Montana and Bennington College, and lives in Billings with her husband and two sons.

Brownies:

1 cup (2 sticks) softened **butter**

2 cups **sugar**

1$\frac{1}{2}$ cups **flour**

1 teaspoon **salt**

$\frac{5}{8}$ cup **cocoa**

2 teaspoons **vanilla**

4 **eggs**, beaten

2 teaspoons **cinnamon**

1 cup **semisweet chocolate chips**

Optional icing:

6 tablespoons softened **butter**

$\frac{1}{2}$ cup **cocoa**

2$\frac{2}{3}$ cups **confectioners' sugar**

1 teaspoon **cinnamon**

$\frac{1}{3}$ cup **evaporated milk**

1 teaspoon **vanilla**

Makes 36 brownies.

MYSTERIOUS BROWNIES

The mystery ingredient in these classic chocolate treats has nothing to do with Alice B. Toklas! It's street legal—only cinnamon! But don't tell your guests—let them figure out the secret for themselves.

Brownies:

1. Preheat oven to 350°.

2. Mix all ingredients except chips in a large bowl.

3. Beat 3 minutes until mixed. Batter will be thick. Do not overbeat.

4. Fold in chips.

5. Spread batter into greased 9-inch by 13-inch pan. Bake for 28 to 30 minutes. Take care not to overbake.

Optional icing:

1. Cream butter in mixing bowl.

2. Combine cocoa, sugar, and cinnamon.

3. Add dry mix alternately with evaporated milk to butter. Beat until smooth, then add vanilla. Add more milk if necessary. Spread over brownies.

From *Blue Wolf*, published by Walker & Company in 2001.

When Dutch Abbott called a couple hours later, I didn't hesitate to shut down the deserted gallery and hightail it out of town. It was a Tuesday, the air held the nostalgia of warm fires and deep forest secrets, and the sky was clear enough to write on…

The cabin had the same feel as Queen's, solitary, cozy, the last bastion of the West's true personality. The man—or woman—alone, needing nothing but a bushel of apples, a cord of wood, and a friendly horse. Or in this case, a pickup truck. Before I reached the top of the porch's four steps, the door opened. From his stooped shoulders the old man peered at me, his white eyebrows low.

"You the nosy one Danny told me about?"

"That's me. Alix Thorssen."

"Thought you'd be a man."

"Are you disappointed?"

"What's in the bag?"

"Apples. And three Hershey bars."

"Chocolate? Who you been talking to? Get your behind in this door. Pronto, girl." He shooed me past him into the cabin. "I got some tea brewing. You take whiskey in yours?"

"I'm trying to go straight."

Dutch hobbled over to the motherly wood stove, where a kettle stood steaming. "I got only one kind of tea. No choices."

I set the bag on the table. "Danny tells me you've lived here all your life."

"And then some. You gonna get out that chocolate or not?"

Lise McClendon has written 6 mysteries, including 4 in the Alix Thorssen series set in Jackson Hole, Wyoming. Two books feature Dorie Lennox, a private eye in World War II–era Kansas City. McClendon lives in Billings, Montana.

1 pint **huckleberries**

2 pints **bing cherries, rhubarb,** or **other fruit** (fresh, frozen, or canned)

$\frac{1}{2}$ cup plus 2 tablespoons **sugar** or **Splenda**, depending on fruit's sweetness

1 tablespoon **lemon juice**

2 tablespoons **minute tapioca**

2 cups **flour**

1 tablespoon **baking powder**

$\frac{1}{2}$ cup **butter**, softened

1 **egg**

$\frac{1}{3}$ cup **milk**

2 tablespoons **sugar**

HUCKLEBERRY COBBLER
(courtesy of Mother Rowland)

1. Preheat oven to 425° and butter a 9-inch by 13-inch baking dish.

2. Combine fruits.

3. Add at least $\frac{1}{2}$ cup sugar and taste for sweetness. Rhubarb, for example, requires more sugar than the other fruits.

4. Add lemon juice and tapioca.

5. Spoon the fruit mixture in buttered pan and put in the hot oven to heat completely before the top is added.

6. Combine flour and baking powder. With your hands or a pastry cutter, work in butter until it is the consistency of coarse crumbs.

7. Beat egg with milk and gently stir into the flour mixture. Knead lightly, adding a bit more flour if it is sticky instead of smooth.

8. Spoon dough onto fruit to completely cover surface and smooth. Sprinkle sugar on the top.

9. Bake for 35 to 45 minutes until browned. If you use fresh rhubarb, make sure it is done.

10. Serve hot, with vanilla ice cream or whipped cream.

○○

From *In Open Spaces*, published by HarperCollins Publishers in 2002.

That night I soaked in a city that was bigger than the combined size of every town I'd ever visited. It was a clear night, five or ten degrees warmer than it would be in Montana, and although I was exhausted, I wanted to absorb as much as I could before I collapsed.

I walked through downtown Omaha, and was struck by the shops—shops that sold only hats or only candy. I couldn't imagine how they stayed in business selling just one product. And the clothes on display in the windows! I wondered where people wore such clothes. But as evening fell, people wearing those very clothes filled the streets, strolling at a leisurely pace. I had to remind myself not to stare, especially at the women, who were glorious in their sleek dresses and stylish hats. Their faces were as smooth and clear as windows, as though they'd never seen an hour of sunlight. And their lips, painted red, looked like cherries in snow. I wanted to turn and follow them.

On the streets, handbills were posted everywhere, and I stopped and read them all. Posters of Calvin Coolidge and John William Davis were pasted to walls and fences, as were pictures of the Nebraska gubernatorial candidates, and other distinguished-looking candidates for lesser offices, looking stern and serious, with slogans circling their heads. There were bills for performances—music, theater, dance, and ads for all kinds of household items, which reminded me of my brother Jack and his schemes to make a quick dollar. But one poster stopped me dead in my tracks. It was for a Negro League baseball game, an exhibition between the Omaha Monarchs and the Mobile Tigers, scheduled for eleven o'clock the next morning. I had a pencil and a notepad in my

jacket, and I wrote down the details. I had called Mr. Murphy, the baseball scout, when I checked into my hotel, and we had made arrangements to meet later in the afternoon. So I would easily be able to make it to the game.

Back at the hotel, I ate in the dining room—shrimp, breaded with crisp batter, and whipped potatoes, and buttery string beans. I'd never tasted shrimp, and although the slippery texture was strange at first, I immediately fell in love with the combination of intense fish flavor and butter-soaked flakes of breading. After a dish of chocolate ice cream, one of my favorite things, I retreated to my room bloated and content.

I took a bath in a real ceramic tub, and slid between sheets thick as cowhide. In my room were electric lights, a toilet, and a sink with running water, none of which we had at home. And the next day, I would be handling the biggest business transaction of my life. But none of those things mattered that night. There were only two things on my mind as I lay on the verge of a deep sleep— my first professional baseball game, and my tryout. I knew that the next day could entirely change my life.

Russell Rowland was born in Bozeman, graduated from Billings West High School, and recently moved back to Missoula, Montana. His first novel, *In Open Spaces*, was loosely based on the lives of his grandparents, who owned a ranch in Carter County. Ivan Doig called the novel "a vivid and distinctive piece of homespun to take its proper place in the literary quilt of the West." Rowland has taught at Boston University, Saint Mary's College, and online with the Gotham Writing Workshop, and is a MacDowell Fellow. He recently completed the sequel to *In Open Spaces*, entitled *The Watershed Years*.

The filling:

1 pint fresh of thawed **blueberries**

1 tablespoon **flour**

Dash of **salt**

½ cup **sugar**

2 tablespoons **lemon juice**

The topping:

1 cup **flour**

1 cup regular **oatmeal**

½ cup brown **sugar**

½ teaspoon **vanilla**

1 cup **butter** or **margarine**

Dash of **salt**

BLUEBERRY CRUNCH

This recipe was always our family's favorite treat when we visited my parents, Truman and Mayetta Smith—well, actually it was the second-best next to my mom's Toll House Cookies!

1. Combine filling ingredients and spread in greased, 8-inch by 8-inch baking pan.

2. Combine dry ingredients.

3. Using hands or a pastry cutter, cut in butter until mixture becomes mealy. Add vanilla.

4. Spread this mixture over blueberries.

5. Bake at 350° for 30 to 40 minutes.

6. Serve warm with vanilla ice cream.

This recipe was previously printed in A Touch of Home: A Collection of Favorite Family Recipes, *which my sister-in-law Carol Power Gilluly compiled for members of the Hart and Gilluly families.*

From a chapter I wrote for *Cooking by the Book: Food in Literature & Culture*, edited by Mary Anne Schofield and published by the Popular Press in 1989.

Authors who attempt to re-create the westering experience in their works have long recognized that the mention of certain foodstuffs can suggest an earlier time or period or a specific region of the country. Thus a novel dealing with a wagon train might contain references to molasses, side pork, jerky, barrels of flour, and other items readers associate with the pioneer era. Careful readings of a number of first-hand and fictional accounts of this period suggest, however, that references to the preparation and offering of food can do more than evoke images of life in the 1800s or early 1900s; they can speak to the emotional state of the women who do the cooking. In a time when provisions were frequently scarce and anything other than the simplest meal demanded foresight and extra effort on the part of the cook, what better way to illustrate a woman's love—or lack thereof—than through her culinary creations?

…[V]isitors at ranch homes and homesteads, whether expected or not, were never sent away hungry. The fare may have been plain, but it was filling.…

Nanny Alderson soon learned that western hospitality…was extended not necessarily by invitation, but whenever a guest arrived at her eastern Montana ranch home. "I would often have to get a meal at odd hours, for one of our own boys or for a visitor who might arrive in the mid-dle of the afternoon after riding fifty miles since breakfast," she recalled in A Bride Goes West. "He'd be hungry and would have to be fed without waiting for supper."

Pioneers relearned cooking beginning with their first nights on the trail when they used an iron pot hung from a tripod above—or simply resting in—a campfire to prepare the family's meals. A.B. Guthrie, Jr., in the Pulitzer Prize-winning The Way West, describes women "wiping smoke tears from their eyes while they tried to settle their cookalls in the flames." Later in the novel, a serious shortage of wood for the cooking fires is encountered; the men of the wagon train meet to consider an important question: Was it right and proper for women to cook over buffalo chips? Such fuel might not be "a ladylike thing" to cook over, but starvation hardly seems a reasonable alternative, and so the unorthodox fuel is approved by the men, although it is decreed that the youngsters, not the women, will collect the chips.

Sue Hart is a professor of English at Montana State University–Billings and a well-known voice on the central and eastern Montana literary scene. She is recipient of a PEN/Syndicated Fiction Award, and a Montana Governor's Humanities Award.

The crust:

16 **graham crackers** *(1 package)*

$\frac{1}{4}$ cup **butter,** melted

$\frac{1}{2}$ cup **sugar**

$\frac{1}{2}$ teaspoon **cinnamon**

The filling:

2 **eggs**

$\frac{1}{3}$ cup **sugar**

$1\frac{1}{2}$ teaspoons **vanilla**

$1\frac{1}{2}$ cups **sour cream**

2 tablespoons **butter,** melted

1 pound **cream cheese**

SOUR CREAM CHEESECAKE

We enjoy a lively potluck scene at the University of Idaho, and this cheesecake is my standard contribution. Faculty and students alike look forward to it. One or two individuals (who shall remain unnamed) have been known, after the last slice has been taken, to pick up the plate and lick it.

The crust:

1. Preheat your oven to 325°.

2. With a rolling pin, crush graham crackers (one of those separately wrapped packages that come in the box of crackers) into fine crumbs.

3. Mix butter, sugar, and cinnamon into the graham cracker crumbs.

4. Press the graham cracker mixture over the bottom and about 2 inches up the sides of a springform pan. Set aside.

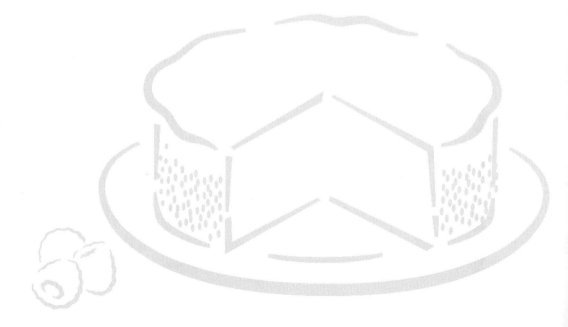

The filling:

1. Put eggs, sugar, vanilla, and sour cream into your blender. Blend for about 30 seconds.

2. Add melted butter and cream cheese to the mixture in the blender and blend for 1 minute or until smooth.

3. Pour batter into springform pan and bake for 35 minutes. Cool and top with fresh fruit (raspberries are especially good).

An excellent variation of this recipe, especially when fresh fruit is out of season, is to substitute 2 teaspoons of almond flavoring for the vanilla and top the cheesecake with a $\frac{1}{2}$ cup slivered almonds.

Mary Clearman Blew is the author of *Sister Coyote: Montana Stories, Bone Deep in Landscape: Writing, Reading and Place, Lambing Out and Other Stories, All but the Waltz,* and the memoir *Balsamroot.* She is also the editor of the recent University of Idaho Press collection *Written on Water: Essays on Idaho Rivers,* and coeditor, with Kim Barnes, of *Circle of Women: An Anthology of Contemporary Western Women's Writing.* Her most recent book, *Writing Her Own Life: Imogene Welch, Western Rural Schoolteacher,* was published in April 2004. A Montana native, Ms. Blew is a professor of English and creative writing at the University of Idaho, Moscow. She has chaired the state humanities councils in both Idaho and Montana.

Andrea Merrill

½ cup **butter**

1 cup **sugar**

2 **eggs,** separated

1 teaspoon **vanilla**

1½ cup sifted **flour**

1 teaspoon **baking powder**

¼ teaspoon **salt**

⅓ cup **milk**

1½ cups fresh **huckleberries**

Andrea Merrill–Maker is the author of *Montana Almanac*, a comprehensive source for information about Big Sky Country, published in 1997 by Falcon Press, Helena, Montana. An updated edition is due in late 2005, published by Globe Pequot Press. She is also the author of a recently published Montana history textbook for grades 4 through 7, *Montana People and Their Stories*, The Grace Dangberg Foundation, Inc., 2004. She is a native of Anaconda, but she currently lives in Missoula, where she recently retired as staff to U.S. Senator Max Baucus.

MELT-IN-YOUR-MOUTH HUCKLEBERRY CAKE

1. Beat butter in large bowl until creamy.

2. Add sugar and beat until fluffy.

3. Beat in egg yolks and vanilla until light and creamy.

4. Sift dry ingredients. Shake a little of the dry ingredients over the berries, so the berries won't sink to the bottom.

5. Add sifted dry ingredients alternately with the milk.

6. Beat egg whites into soft peaks and fold into batter. Fold in fresh berries.

7. Turn into a greased 8-inch by 8-inch pan. Sprinkle top of the batter lightly with granulated sugar. Bake at 350° for 50 to 60 minutes.

From *Montana Almanac*, published by Falcon Press in 1997.

Throughout the 1930s and 1940s, the legendary huckleberry crops of western Montana provided a free food supply and critical economic activity during tough times. Old-timers tell of the great "huckleberry camps," where Indian and white families would bring camping and canning equipment into woods and stay until the berries were gone. In certain good drainages, there were sometimes five hundred tepees, an improvised store, and a general boomtown atmosphere.

MOM'S CHOCOLATE SYRUP

Liza Nicholas

1. In a pot or double boiler, melt butter and chocolate until smooth.

2. Stir in sugar and salt until dissolved.

3. Slowly add milk and then vanilla, stirring continuously until smooth.

4. Serve over ice cream.

$\frac{1}{2}$ cup **butter**

4 squares **unsweetened chocolate**

3 cups **sugar**

$\frac{1}{2}$ teaspoon **salt**

1 can **evaporated milk**

1 tablespoon **vanilla**

Liza Nicholas is the author of *Becoming Western: Stories of Culture and Identity in the Cowboy State*, forthcoming from the University of Nebraska Press, and numerous articles about the West, its people and culture. She is the coeditor of *Imagining the Big Open: Nature, Identity and Play in the New West.* She lives, writes, and teaches in Bozeman, Montana.

The crust:

4 parts **flour**

> **Salt** to taste (¼ teaspoon for 2-crust pie)

2 parts **lard** or **butter**

1 part ice **water**

(If you start with a quart of flour, you'll have enough for 4 9-inch, 2-crust pies.)

The filling:

4 pounds ground or hand-minced **venison** *(or beef),* cooked

½ pound **leaf fat from bison** *(or bear, pork, or beef or, if you're a wimp, 2 cups butter, ground or hand-minced)*

8 pounds **buffalo berries** *(or dried cranberries or fresh or dried apples)*

1 quart **unsweetened apple cider** or **hard cider**

5 pounds **brown sugar**

½ tablespoon **cinnamon**

1 tablespoon **allspice**

½ tablespoon **cloves**

½ teaspoon **nutmeg**

> Pint of **brandy** *(apricot is good),* or whisky will do

ELECTA'S MINCEMEAT PIE

In the mid-1860s the measure of a woman's worth was taken by the quality of the biscuit and the crust of the pie she set on her table.

○○

The crust:

1. Toss sifted flour and salt into a bowl.

2. Divide the shortening into 2 parts.

3. Take half the shortening and work into flour with fingers, 2 knives, or a wire blender, until the mix feels mealy. Add rest of shortening and work until this shortening is pea-sized.

4. Add water and mix with fork until it forms a ball. Pinch off a bit more than a half-cup-sized piece, pat into a ball, toss onto a floured board, pat flat, then roll out until it is about ⅛-inch thick.

5. Slip into pie plate and leave the dough to extend beyond the lip.

6. Pinch off a bit less than a half-cup-sized piece and proceed as above except before you place it on top of the pie, first fold it in half and prick vent holes either with a fork or by making slits on the top with a sharp knife. Place the vented top over the filling and seal the crusts together by pressing the edge with a fork. Trim the excess with a knife then pat the edge of the crust so that it folds just a bit under the pie plate rim. This keeps the crusts from shrinking.

The filling:

1. Mix all ingredients together. This mixture will keep indefinitely in the refrigerator without any detriment to its flavor.

2. However, when the time comes to bake it, put filling in a pie shell and do so for about 35 minutes at 350°. (If you're using a wood stove, the right temperature has been reached when a tablespoon of flour turns brown within 10 minutes of being tossed on the oven floor.) The pie is done when the crust is golden. Serve hot.

The pie shell:

1 cup plus 3 tablespoons **shortening**

3 cups **flour**

1 tablespoon **salt**

1 **egg**, beaten

5 tablespoons cold **water**

1 teaspoon **vinegar**

The filling:

6 or 7 **Golden Delicious apples,** peeled and cored

1 cup **sugar**

1 tablespoon **cinnamon**

$2\frac{1}{2}$ tablespoons **cornstarch**

$\frac{1}{2}$ cup **water**

GRANDMA'S APPLE PIE

Before moving to Montana at the age of 12, I was up to my fourth- or fifth-generation knees in Appalachia, in a little town north of Charleston, West Virginia. My maternal grandparents had 10 kids and 20 or 30 grandkids. Every Sunday, they'd host these enormous dinners. Two or three kinds of meats (fried chicken, roast beef, pork chops), pinto beans, corn bread, a buffet table filled with cakes and pies. My grandmother's apple pie was the best I've ever eaten, and still remains my gold standard for desserts. It's best if it's served hot, and out from under a blue and white checked dishcloth, with a screen door slamming shut as cousins chase each other around the house. An old man should have his feet up in a recliner, complaining about the Republicans, and an old woman should already be tugging you into a backroom to slip you five bucks so you can go buy your girlfriend something nice. Tire swings aren't mandatory but are recommended.

The pie shell:

1. Blend shortening, flour, and salt with a pastry blender.

2. In a bowl, mix egg, water, and vinegar.

3. Add egg mix to flour and mix well.

4. Roll out into a pie shell. Should make enough for 3 single crust pies.

The filling:

1. Chop apples into small pieces.

2. Put in a pot and fill with water almost to top of apples. Add sugar and cinnamon.

3. Bring water to a boil and cook for 2 minutes.

4. Mix cornstarch into $\frac{1}{2}$ cup water and stir into the apples.

5. Scoop out apples and put into your pie shell, adding an appropriate amount of juice from the pot (this is a guess, and only Grandma ever got it really right).

6. Bake at 450° for 15 minutes, then 350° for 35 minutes. After baking, sprinkle cinnamon and sugar over the outer crust.

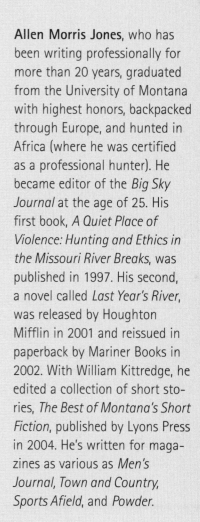

Allen Morris Jones, who has been writing professionally for more than 20 years, graduated from the University of Montana with highest honors, backpacked through Europe, and hunted in Africa (where he was certified as a professional hunter). He became editor of the *Big Sky Journal* at the age of 25. His first book, *A Quiet Place of Violence: Hunting and Ethics in the Missouri River Breaks*, was published in 1997. His second, a novel called *Last Year's River*, was released by Houghton Mifflin in 2001 and reissued in paperback by Mariner Books in 2002. With William Kittredge, he edited a collection of short stories, *The Best of Montana's Short Fiction*, published by Lyons Press in 2004. He's written for magazines as various as *Men's Journal*, *Town and Country*, *Sports Afield*, and *Powder*.

HUCKLEBERRY TART

It's not really summer in Montana for me until the first huckleberries arrive at the Missoula Farmers Market. When the season is at its peak, the market literally reeks of the berries. Montana caviar, I like to call them and, like their aquatic namesake, they carry the potent flavor of their origins—June snowmelt and high-altitude sunshine condensed inside each perfect purple gem. In this simple version of a traditional French raspberry and cream tart, the berries take center stage. Buy 2 pints and stick the extra one in your freezer for huckleberry pancakes. Come January, you'll be happy you did.

The crust:

1 cup all-purpose **flour**

6 tablespoons **unsalted butter,** chilled and cut into pieces

Pinch of **salt**

½ cup **powdered sugar**

1 large **egg**

The filling:

3 large **egg yolks**

3 tablespoons granulated **sugar**

¾ cup **crème fraîche** *(if you can't find crème fraîche, you can substitute with a mixture of half heavy cream and half sour cream)*

1 pint **huckleberries**

Confectioners' sugar for dusting

The crust:

1. With a food processor or pastry cutter, combine the flour, butter, salt, and sugar until the mixture resembles coarse crumbs.

2. Add egg and pulse or mix with a fork until the dough begins to come together.

3. Transfer the dough to waxed paper or plastic wrap and bring it together into a ball, then flatten it into a disc.

4. Dust your fingertips with flour and, working quickly, press the dough into and up the sides of a 10-inch loose-bottomed tart pan. Cover and refrigerate for 2 to 3 hours.

5. Line the pan with aluminum foil and fill with baking weights, rice, or dried beans, to prevent shrinkage. Bake for 20 minutes. Remove the weights and foil and bake for another 20 minutes, or until nicely browned. Set aside to cool before filling.

The filling:
1. Preheat the oven to 375°.

2. Place the egg yolks in a bowl and beat with a fork. Stir in the sugar and crème fraîche and mix until well combined.

3. Place the berries in an even layer in the baked tart shell and pour the egg and cream mixture over them.

4. Bake in the center of the oven just until the filling begins to set, about 15 minutes.

5. Cool, then dust with confectioners' sugar before serving.

Jenny Siler grew up in Missoula, Montana. She has traveled widely and worked as, among other things, a salmon grader, grape picker, furniture mover, forklift driver, and bartender. She now lives in temporary exile in Lexington, Virginia, with her husband and daughter, and writes full-time.

From *Iced*, published by Henry Holt in 2000.

The sun had just gone down when I pulled into a spot by the back door of the Oxford Saloon. It was happy hour at other bars around town, but here, where the atmosphere tends toward perpetual gloom, there were only a few stragglers in the café and some diligent gamblers back in the flickering light of the poker and keno machines.

I found a stool at the counter and ordered a cup of coffee.

"You eating?" the waitress asked. She looked relieved when I shook my head no.

I watched her trundle down the far end of the counter and return to her copy of *People* magazine.

The coffee was strong and bitter, the dregs of a pot that undoubtedly had been cooking away since that morning. But it was hot and I was bone-cold and happy to have it. I lit a cigarette and looked up at the back-lit menu board above the grill. BRAINS AND EGGS, the sign read, and then, in parentheses, BECAUSE HE NEEDS 'EM.

GRILLED FRUIT

When my friend Charles Perry, the distinguished food historian who writes for the Los Angeles Times, *came up to Montana for a visit one year, I prepared the following dessert. He'd just finished an article on grilling and phoned his editor the next day.*

"Have we gone to press yet?" he asked. "No. OK, you know where I said you can't successfully grill fruit? Let's lose that sentence."

○○○

4 **apples** or **pears**

3 tablespoons **butter**, melted

2 tablespoons **sugar**

Dash of **cinnamon**

Serves 4 to 8, depending on appetites. You know best.

To grill fruit:

1. Prepare a grill for direct heat.

2. Half and core four apples or pears. (Some people may want to peel the fruit: I don't find that necessary, but it's a nice touch.)

3. Toss the fruit in a bowl with butter and sugar. (I like a little cinnamon on the apples as well.)

4. Grill the fruit, cut side down, over direct heat, turning once or twice. It takes anywhere from 10 to 20 minutes. The fruit is ready when it is easily pierced with a thin-bladed knife. The apples and pears should be lightly browned and show grill marks. It takes a couple of go-rounds to know exactly how you like them and when to take them off the fire.

Cooking notes: Use more sugar and the fruit will look more charred. Some people think that looks cool and others find that all that black caramelized sugar is not to their taste. Err on the side of less sugar to start. Or don't use any sugar at all, just butter, and the fruit makes a great side for any pork dish.

For dessert, I like the fruit just as it comes off the grill. More fastidious cooks than I might make a lemon cream sauce or used whipped cream to top the fruit. If I feel the need, I put some vanilla ice cream I've allowed to soften a bit in the fruit where the core used to be.

Softer summer fruits, like peaches, take less time. On the other hand, the peaches I can buy in Montana often seem to be made of granite. They take longer. Grilling softens them and brings out the flavor.

My friend, Jim Liska, who owns the Adagio Restaurant in Livingston, has modified this recipe and makes a popular dessert of grilled peaches and fresh basil served over softened ice cream.

From *Hold the Enlightenment*, hardcover published by Villard Books, a division of Random House in 2002; paperback by Vintage Departures in 2003.

Traditionally, in the ranching and farming communities of the West and mid-West, lutefisk dinners are served in Lutheran churches during winter, just before Christmas. The word "lutefisk" means "lyefish," which refers to the ancient Viking process of drying fish and soaking it in poisonous lye to preserve it.

Lutefisk, as served at the Lutheran functions, won't actually kill you, though there is a rumor that, in the small rural town of Wilsall, lye-soaked scraps were left out in back of the church and that cows from a nearby field got through the fence, ate the fish, and died. In fact, I called the distributor of the lutefisk used there and he assured me that the Olsen Fish Company buys its dried cod direct from Norway, "lutes it," then sends it through several rinses. When a customer receives a shipment, it is free of toxicity and ready to boil and eat. So the rumor of cows dying from eating lye is entirely false.

They died from eating lutefisk.

Tim Cahill is the author of at least 8 books, including, most recently, *Lost in My Own Backyard*, published by Crown Publishing Group in 2004. He is a founding editor of *Outside* magazine and writes frequently for national publications.

Dorothy Hinshaw Patent

MOTHER'S APPLESAUCE SLICES

This is an updated version of what my mother called "apple sauce." Some might refer to this as stewed apples. Her version consisted of lovely, intact apple slices in a heavy, sweet syrup. I can still feel the grains of powdered cinnamon on my tongue when I think of sitting in the breakfast nook eating a bowl of Mother's sauce. The pinch of salt is my grandfather's touch. I've modified the recipe by using cinnamon sticks instead of powdered cinnamon and fresh cider for the liquid. I've also used a minimum amount of extra sugar so the flavor of the apples isn't drowned out by sweetness. If you use a sweeter variety of apple, such as Roxbury Russet, you won't need to add any sugar at all. This dish is very versatile—it makes a good breakfast fruit, after-school snack, or children's dessert. It is best served warm. The recipe can be doubled easily.

1 pound *(2 large)* **Granny Smith apples**, quartered, cored, peeled, and sliced into $\frac{1}{8}$-inch wedges

2 cups fresh **apple cider**

One 3-inch **cinnamon stick**

Pinch of **salt**

Makes about 3 cups

1. Place the apples in a medium saucepan, along with the other ingredients.

2. Cover the pan and bring the mixture to a boil over medium-high heat. Uncover the pan, stir the apples gently, and lower the heat to medium.

3. Simmer, partially covered, until the apples are translucent and tender, about 20 minutes. Stir frequently to make sure the slices cook evenly.

4. Cool slightly and serve warm.

Variations: *Add some dried cranberries to the apples as they cook for tanginess and color. A little freshly grated ginger adds liveliness. Fuji apples, cooked in orange juice instead of cider, are a good combination. For a chunky applesauce, break up the slices into small to medium pieces with a wooden spoon or potato masher.*

From "Snow White and the Poisoned Apple" in *An Apple a Day* by Greg Patent and Dorothy Hinshaw Patent, published by Broadway Books in 1999.

We are all familiar with the fairy tale of Snow White. Today the version in the Disney movie is probably the best known. But how does it compare to the original? The story of Snow White is ancient, having been passed down orally through countless generations. No one knows how many versions exist, but folklorists have compared as many as a hundred at a time. Thus, no one can lay claim to knowing the "original" version. During the 1800s, the Grimm brothers in Germany collected oral tales and put them into books, setting in print limited versions of these old tales.

...The death of the queen comes in at least three different ways. In the old Grimm versions, she dances herself to death in heated iron shoes. In my childhood book, she breaks her magic mirror in fury at finding out Snow White is alive and marrying the prince, and she falls dead as the mirror smashes. In the movie, she falls off a cliff to her death.

Interestingly, one constant through at least many of the version is the poisoned apple, bright red and too tempting to be resisted. Can we say the same about a modern Red Delicious?

Dorothy Hinshaw Patent was born in Rochester, Minnesota, and grew up in Marin County, California. She always loved nature and received a BA in biological sciences from Stanford University and an MA and PhD in zoology from the University of California, Berkeley. While she was a graduate student, she met and married Greg Patent. They have two grown sons with wonderful wives and four delightful grandchildren. They lived in a number of places, including Naples, Italy, before settling in Missoula in 1972, the same year Dorothy began her writing career. Montana has provided topics for many of her books, including ones on wolves, bison, and Lewis and Clark. Over the last 30-plus years, she has written more than 130 books, mostly science and nature books for children, as well as 2 gardening books for adults. She coauthored a cookbook, *A is for Apple*, with her husband. This recipe is from that book.

Deirdre McNamer

½ cup **butter**

1 cup **sugar**

1 cup **flour**

⅛ teaspoon **salt**

2 teaspoons **baking powder**

½ cup **milk**

1 package **frozen raspberries** *(the old-fashioned kind with the syrup if you can find them)* or 1½ cups frozen berries, defrosted, sugared to taste, juice reserved

Serves 4 or 5.

Deirdre McNamer is the author of the novels *Rima in the Weeds, One Sweet Quarrel,* and *My Russian.* She is an associate professor of fiction at the University of Montana.

GREAT-AUNT GLADYS'S RASPBERRY PUDDING

1. Cream butter. Add ½ cup sugar and cream until light.

2. Add sifted dry ingredients in a couple of small batches, alternating with milk.

3. Pour into buttered 8-inch by 8-inch pan.

4. Sprinkle remaining ½ cup sugar over.

5. Pour berries and juice over all.

6. Bake 350° for 45 minutes. Serve warm with cream.

From "Water Thieves," published in *Ploughshares* in 2002.

The spice rub seared the crab-shell cut in her thumb. She swore at it, then washed her hands and refocused. Pork: rubbed well and chilling docilely. Ditto the mixture for the crab cakes (sauteed peppers and onion, mustard, parsley, mayonnaise, lemon juice, Tabasco, bread crumbs, the crabmeat). Small red potatoes had roasted in a mustard vinaigrette; beans were blanched and cooling.

She was running behind. The rest of them were due back at four, and she didn't want to be messing with the Key lime pie when they got in, so she made the crust and baked it, whipped the filling together, and into the fridge it went, looking runnier than she would have liked. Set up, you little shit, she whispered.

Index

○○○